Holistic Active Management of Non-Performing Loans

Claudio Scardovi

Holistic Active Management of Non-Performing Loans

Springer

Claudio Scardovi
AlixPartners
London
UK

ISBN 978-3-319-25362-6 ISBN 978-3-319-25363-3 (eBook)
DOI 10.1007/978-3-319-25363-3

Library of Congress Control Number: 2015954354

Springer Cham Heidelberg New York Dordrecht London

Printed on acid-free paper

Springer International Publishing AG Switzerland is part of Springer Science+Business Media (www.springer.com)

Acknowledgments

Special thanks to Dina Siena, Valentina Proverbio, Paolo Pucino and Giuseppe Farinacci for their continued support and help in the development of this book.

Contents

Chapter 1
Work-Out: Holistic Active Management of NPL

Abstract Non Performing Loans (NPLs) have become a hot issue after the global financial crisis that started in 2008, currently under discussion in many fora and institutional instances, as far as they are considered to be an important factor jeopardizing the lending capacity of European banks. In this chapter a definition of NPLs is provided, as long as a brief synopsis of the overall structure of the handbook and of its learning objects, starting from the technical analysis of the potential solutions to NPLs management and work out and of their main pros and cons to be considered.

Keywords Non performing loans · NPLs · Europe · European banks · Workout

1.1 Introduction

Credit work out (or credit recovery, or credit collection) management is one of the oldest activities on earth. It is indeed as old as the credit business itself since, unfortunately, bad creditors (and bad bankers) have quite likely always existed.

While in the financial literature there are many definitions that can be used to identify what a recovery process is, this book will mostly focus on workout seen as the science and the art of maximizing the potential total recovered value coming from a troubled, non performing situation—and taking into consideration the situation of the bad creditor as well. Under this perspective in fact, the non-performing counterpart has still to be considered as a "client" and be treated as such, as he shares just part of the blame for the distressed situation. Indeed other counterparts have to be held responsible as well, starting from the bank which, leaving aside situations associated with fraud, also made a mistake in allocating an unsustainable portion of credit to the customer (and the too risky business case associated with his investment and consumption decisions) in the first place.

Following this hypothesis, the end product of credit work out is therefore to reach an optimal closing of the situation, maximizing the value for the bank,

C. Scardovi, *Holistic Active Management of Non-Performing Loans*,
DOI 10.1007/978-3-319-25363-3_1

while at the same time making sure that the relationship with the customer is maintained—if and when appropriate—and that the business interests and the economy as a whole have to suffer as little disruption as possible.

While credit work out may, at a first glance, appear an old and un-sexy activity, recent developments in the volume of non-performing loans have made this an incredibly relevant and even fashionable topic. In fact, because of the global financial crisis and the subsequent European economic slowdown, it has become a super critical issue, as it is key for the restructuring, turnaround and transformation of the European banking system and for the re-launch and development of the European economy. By restoring the situation of banks to a steady state, an effective workout will have a significant impact on the lives of many small businesses and mid and large sized corporates and on millions of retail customers. Firstly, workout is key to the recovery of the stability and safety of the global financial system and for the full repairing of banks' balance sheet; secondly, it can contribute to the recovery of profitability in banks, which are currently still under water because the mistakes they made in the past still out-weight the changes that have been put in place to put a remedy to them. Reshaping banks' balance sheets and making some clarity over them, will in turn prompt the liberation of entrapped resources and their optimal re-allocation in the economy, as it creates transparency and further information and intelligence on what went wrong, liberating the remaining value of sub or non performing assets that could then end up being traded on relatively liquid and transparent secondary markets. Finally, credit workout is key for the "creative destruction" process, which does not only involve financial assets and their underlying collaterals (including real estate and equipment assets), but the same banks that originated them.

However, given the current status of such activity, there are still quite critical missing pieces to reach an effective "WHAM" (a work out management which is both holistic and active in nature, and "smart", as it was, for the aficionados, the "pop" music group lead in the eighties by George Michael). As such, we highlight how the holistic approach we suggest should consider all kinds of strategies, selecting a different solution depending on the specific situation, instead of limiting the analysis to the segmentation of credits or clients; and be very much focused on an "active" approach that tries to shorten as much as possible the time to recovery of any such strategies.

These strategies can involve judicial, non judicial or mixed approaches, but the ultimate goal is always to optimize the stakeholders' value involved. This, in turn, entails implementing a sort of copernican revolution by which NPLs move from being a neglected dead weight to becoming a more structural (and anyway unavoidable, even in good times) component of the banks. Indeed, they constitute the centerpiece of a whole "solvency system" and have to be analyzed in its integrity. Such comprehensive analysis will in turn allow to capture the true essence of the loan, regardless of how complex it might be, and to assess the appropriate method to deal with it. For example, a bank will be able to classify a client having many credit products, as being corporate or retail, or being part of a cluster of companies and of an economic value chain affecting sub-suppliers and employees in a certain way—e.g. understanding and anticipating the potential follow on effects.

A holistic view can also promote a greater focus on the collateral: whether it is a real estate asset, equipment or a simple third party guarantee, a troubled debtor could potentially get back to work and recover his solvency. In this sense, the role of the bank is to treat its counterparty as a true "client", in the sense that it will provide him assistance in order to effectively enable him to become solvent again (or at least to repay as much as possible the amount which has become overdue).

Ultimately, the active/proactive view suggests that the key missing point in continental Europe relates to speed—an even more critical issue, given the current macroeconomic scenarios dominated by low or negative inflation which is not even helping the accounting impacts of any "wait and see" strategy. Indeed, if a timely action is not undertaken, European banks will have to forego the possibility of ever achieving a full or even satisfactory recovery, as once value is lost, it will not get back. The urgency of the task explains why this credit recovery is therefore all about being "fast and furious", and an art as much as a science, as the ultimate price is the value that allows the bank, and its related system (shareholders, employees, clients and other troubled debtors included) to survive.

1.2 An Overview of the Book

In this book, we will start our discussion of the "WHAM" approach to credit work out from a Chap. 2 dedicated to the analysis of the concept of non-performing loans. Despite the nowadays increasing importance of such topic, there is still no precise, univocally used definition of what a non-performing loan is. Therefore, we will try, in the Chap. 2, to give an overview of what are the possible definitions of an overdue loan, collecting the interpretation given by regulators, practitioners and other market players. The importance of such definition is that it could allow a more precise and applicable classification of loans, consequentially limiting discrepancies among countries and also various phenomena of hiding and misclassification of the same assets. Moreover, a clearer identification of those that are sub or not performing should help banks in taking a more proactive approach and tackle them through an efficient workout strategy. This chapter will also go on analyzing what are the key drivers of the recent trend started with the spread of the global financial crisis that have seen non performing loans multiplying their weight on banks' balance sheets. The analysis will also address banks' specific factors such as their low capitalization and limited profitability usually associated with great amount of NPLs on their books.

The impact of the accumulation of non-performing loans in banks' balance sheets is in fact not only a matter of lower profitability due to recurrent write-offs, but also a mismatch one between the interests paid by the banks on liabilities and the forgone interests on loans on the asset side. This phenomenon, together with the information asymmetry naturally embedded in such opaque portfolios, could turn into a liquidity, or even into a solvency problem for banks. The common (very troublesome) methods to deal with the issue of non performing loans accumulation span then from "evergreening" to entering riskier activities to compensate for the losses. Given the potential systemic effects of such actions, we consider the alternative method of creating a "ctedir work out unit" holistically and proactively focused on the active recovery of such loans. Since this topic is gaining more and more attention, we analyze some examples of recent creations of "credit work out" units (sometimes also dubbed "bad banks"—a misnoumer in so many ways) in Europe and put them into the "WHAM" approach perspective.

Chapter 3 will deal instead with the analysis of the so called "credit lifecycle". We aim at describing how the lifecycle of bank's loans works and how they move from a phase to the other. We will then take a look at what happens to the loans before they eventually become non performing—the real focus of this book. In fact, in our view, a bank has to be able to manage loans in an active way at each one of the stages and staring from the beginning, in order to optimize as much as possible the recovery performance of NPLs. For each stage, we will identify critical thresholds and a specific management approaches, from origination, to ongoing servicing, to recovery. The approach that we suggest to effectively manage a credit portfolio—from inception to closure—is an approach of specialization, usually developed through the segmentation of such portfolio. Given that the bank has thousands of defaulted exposures, it is necessary to be able to organize them into homogenous portfolios of similar loans from the very beginning, starting from the gathering and accumulation of the proper data sets that are most useful for any of the identified cluster. In fact, credit portfolios can be segmented using few key drivers such as ticket size, vintage, presence of third party guarantee, kind of collateral etc. and in a pretty straightforward way—but separately for banking and leasing exposures. Any of these key drivers is then sub segmented into few buckets, so that the number of possible permutations increases. For any of these permutations, a detailed analysis of the best strategies to manage credits and the smartest ways to build consistent capabilities can be defined, also based on the detailed analysis of the associated economics.

Chapter 4 of this book addresses the organizational challenge of defining the best approach to follow in order to deal with NPLs. This issue concerns mainly the decision around the optimal level of externalization for the bank. Each portfolio of loans—as defined by the clusterization procedure described in the previous chapter, has to be taken care of through a specific workout approach. We recognize that two mains set ups are possible: captive (e.g. using a credit work out as a fully embedded unit or as a distinct company fully owned by the bank) or non-captive (e.g. via a joint venture, alliance or through a third party commercial relationship—basically outsourcing the recovery activities). For each setup, we give an overview on the model and on the possible advantages as well as drawbacks. The selection of the appropriate setup is then driven by three main factors: the ownership of the assets, the center of responsibility for the recovery activities and the role of the workout unit in terms of contribution to the profit and loss of the bank. We then discuss the concept of an "alpha player" credit work out platform, able to recover more than the market average, whatever the economic cycle and market conditions. The "alpha player" concept is then used to discuss whilst more traditional approaches are focussing only on cost minimization—thus leading to sub-optimized recovery rates—other, more innovative and "alpha playing" approach are focussing on the recovery maximization, decreasing the cost of risk as their main strategic target.

Chapter 5 is then focused on the practical steps that a bank should take in order to set up a credit workout unit. The key point is that a holistic and active credit workout unit has to be designed and built in order to reflect the market best practice and bring a consistent benefit to the bank itself. Therefore, we want to define what are the key milestones and the essential pillars that must be implemented to obtain an efficient credit workout unit. Firstly we concentrate on the steps aimed at designing and creating the unit. Synthetically, this part of the process involves the diagnostic of the current situation concerning the portfolios of NPLs, through the help of a significant and well-constructed database, a well designed dashboard and credit segmentation approach, the definition of an operating model and the full build up of the unit. Then, the bank has also to consider whether to implement crash programs to identify those positions that need urgent attention, whilst the overall "best in class" platform is being built. In our discussion, we focus also on the possible accelerators to the credit recovery overall strategy—mainly focusing on the real estate underlying collaterals.

Chapter 6 is then focussing on the potential impacts that NPL portfolios on the banks' balance sheets can have. Since the workout process, as analyzed in the previous chapter, requires investments and resources, the bank has to evaluate if it has the right set of capabilities that make it possible to be an active player, able to outplay third parties in recovery effectiveness and if the recovery potential is enough to cover the costs incurred. Therefore, we analyze the value that the NPL portfolios would have if managed by different parties. Then, we focus on the analysis of the different recovery strategies. For this scope, it is necessary to set up an appropriate database that would allow to subdivide NPLs into portfolios and then later on to define a specialized strategy to tackle each one of them. The valuation of each portfolio has to take into consideration two main dimensions: the value "as is", that is the embedded value of a portfolio also considering elements as the collateral or the external guarantees; and the value "to be", after the workout process. After having determined a valuation for each portfolio under different sets of assumption, it is then possible to define the optimal recovery strategy. This is done by confronting the Net Present Value of each portfolio with its fair value, market and liquidation value—and the different hypothesis of recovery strategy underpinning any of such scenarios. It will be then possible to determine if the current recovery strategy is confirmed, revised or will need substantial changes.

Chapter 7 is then dedicated to the execution of such value maximization strategies, taking into account what can be done internally by the bank's captive credit work out and what is, instead, better outsourced to third parties. In any case, a continuous focus has to be put on managing competitively the internal resources of the bank, and on managing competitively all the third parties that will be used through time for externalizing some part or most of the recovery value chain.

A specific section will then be dedicated to the monitoring, controlling of these third parties credit work out unit and to their most effective incentivization through time.

On the following, Chap. 8, we briefly address another important element of banks' balance sheets and discuss sub performing corporate loans. The approach on sub performing corporate loans is different given the fact that, differently from NPLs whose recovery value is mainly driven by the collateral, their value is still anchored to the health, both financial and industrial, of the company as an ongoing concern. Therefore the bank should constantly monitor and assess the situation of the counterpart, in order to prevent and identify proactively the situations on which to intervene. Generally the strategies that a bank can pursue on a sub performing loan are two: sell the loan (reducing the exposure by transferring these assets to other financial investors) or proactively manage its related risks through moral suasion and good advice. We therefore analyze all the main strategic options that the bank has to play in order to either prevent the company's failure (with the help of third party consultants focused on cash management and operational and business turnaround—that should be hired by the company itself, not by the bank) or to limit the losses stemming out of a terminally troubled situation, at the light of its almost inevitable bankruptcy.

On Chap. 9, we analyze another sector that is deeply interconnected with the banking business—the real estate sector and with specific reference to the development phase of its life cycle. In fact, the most widly used collateral for loans in banking is a real estate asset. Therefore banks should develop internal skills and proper strategies to deal with this particular asset category—and even more so when the clients being financed are real estate developers. Numerous are the instruments that could be used by banks; and we distinguish between those that can be implemented when the bank still does not have the property of the assets, therefore by moral suasion only (through such approaches as what we call "AREM—active real estate management"; or the "real estate agency"), from those that are characterized by a direct management of the assets because the bank is already the direct owner. We also mention "ASM—active space management" techniques, which are meant to allow to the bank the identification of the steps needed to optimize the output and minimize the inputs on owned real estate assets, therefore increasing their productivity and financial yield. By implementing these kind of actions the bank could in fact operate both on its cost of risk and on its profitability, and ideally in an integrated and consistent way.

Chapter 10 deals with the management of a special category of NPL portfolios, linked to leasing equipment loans. The peculiarity of these leasing contracts is that, differently from any banking loans, the bank is already the owner of the collateral asset since the beginning of the contract. The key point the chapter is making is about the centrality of the role that a collateral has for this kind of contracts—particularly when when assessing the recovery value and the best remarketing strategies leading to the final collection. Given the fact that the collaterals greatly vary in nature and characteristics, the recovery strategy will not be unique but will be specifically designed to optimally address each asset's features. By identifying the optimal strategy to manage each leasing equipment class, banks should then be able to recover as much value as possible from its NPL leasing portfolio and from its remarketing activities.

The last chapter of the book is finally is finally addressing two main topics. The first one discusses how the concept of industrialization could be applied to banks' loans credit work out activities. The industrialization of the credit collection of banks impacts mostly on the operating model of credit work out platforms and it consists in implementing a holistic approach to the build up and management of their recovery capabilities, so that to optimize the productivity derived from them (e.g. the level of output—the recovered value, obtained per any input—the cost of recovery, used in this process). The second topic of this chapter is then centered on the most innovative approaches designed to address the NPLs problem in a more "creative" way. As we will see, credit workout is a sort of "must do" activity for the bank that drives significant costs and heavy usage of resources. However, credit work out is not just a purgatory or a necessary evil, but could become a source of value creation if performed in innovative ways and developing capabilities and services which could become, in turn, marketable to third parties at a price. The generation of value could derive from a number of different sources—let's call them adjacent businesses. And the real innovation stands in the fact that NPLs are not treated anymore just as a dead weight to either hide or get rid of, but assume a central role in the bank's core business—potentially, even as a new revenues generating business opportunity, as described in the closing remarks of the book.

Chapter 2
The Bad Bank and the Good Banking

Abstract Non Performing Loans (NPLs) may arise in response to micro (e.g. and improper bank's corporate governance and very poor risk and lending policies) and/or macro factors (e.g. deep and prolonged recession in the "real economy" of a certain Country) and the analysis and understanding of both may help in understanding recent events and maybe predict future ones. When NPLs are becoming so relevant to potentially impair the lending supply, systemic "bad bank" solutions could be explored as last resort options to avert the meltdown of the financial system. Ireland and Spain have developed recently strong programs to clean their banks' balance sheets, whilst others (e.g. Italy) are still considering the opportunity of such scheme and the most proper way to allow some kind of public intervention (as allowed by current UE State-Aid regulation). In extreme cases, a "bad bank" can prove quite effective and quite a "good thing".

Keywords NPL definition · NPL market · Bad bank · Ireland · Spain · Public intervention

2.1 What NPL Really Means

As we have seen, NPLs are a natural and unavoidable component of the balance sheet of any bank, but following the financial crisis they have moved from being a physiological element to becoming a pathological problem. Since 2008, non-performing loans have been an increasingly hot topic in the international scene, due to their important and rising volume and their impact on the economy as a whole, on the banking system and on its credit supply.

As a start, NPLs lack of a regulatory framework and an internationally accepted standard for their assessment. This means that there is no precise and univocal interpretation of loan classification; therefore many different categorizations are in force and may vary from country to country. According to the New Capital Accord of Basel II, introduced in 2007, NPLs are those whose interest and principal

C. Scardovi, *Holistic Active Management of Non-Performing Loans*,
DOI 10.1007/978-3-319-25363-3_2

payments are past due for more than 90 days or for which there is a good reason to consider that these payments will never be made in full. It is important to notice that the definition provided considers NPLs gross of provisions and accounts for the total amount of defaulted outstanding loans. A still high level definition of defaulted loans distinguishes then between non performing loans and sub performing loans. These last are the ones that have already defaulted but still do not meet Basel II requirements to be considered non performing. A further sub segmentation can be found by identifying watch list loans, that are performing loans with a high probability of defaulting in the upcoming future and an internal rating equal or worse than B.

Despite the fact that the 90 days overdue rule is generally applied, national regulators tend finally to differ in the standards of measurement of NPLs and in their treatment of aspects such as the collateral, the restructured loans and the multiple loans by the same defaulted borrower. Therefore, local interpretation of the general definitions leaves plenty of room in the classification of loans. Moreover, we must take into consideration the difficulties of the regulators in enforcing a homogenous NPL reporting by banks. As an example, in Italy impaired loans are sub classified by the Bank of Italy as: "scaduti"—loans past due for more than 90 days; "ristrutturati"—in case the bank has agreed in applying some structural modifications on the loan in order to facilitate the repayment; "incagli"—watchlist loans, those characterized by a persisting, difficult situation of the creditor but still considered by the bank as holding a probability of recovery; "sofferenze"—loans that the bank has to consider irrecoverable and never to be paid. However these differences and sub categories are soon to be abandoned following the European Banking Authority (EBA) implementation of a unique definition of forbearance and non-performing exposure.

2.2 Perception, Deception

It is useful to underline that the European Security and Market Authority (ESMA) in December 2012 stressed the importance of transparency and of an appropriate and consistent application of measurement and recognition standards as indicated by the IFRS (international financial reporting standards). A study this last one conducted on a sample of European listed financial institutions showed how disclosure about forbearance practices in financial statements can vary significantly. Moreover it highlighted that, since write offs under IFRS regulation are relatively flexible, comparison across banks may be difficult. Summing up, the main difficulties in comparing different banks on the amount, the measurement and classification of loans they hold as non performing are related to three main aspects that should be carefully taken in consideration and analyzed in order to have a fully and truly representative view of the event:

- First of all, there could be lack of consistency across countries concerning the classification of NPLs, since there are differences in accounting approaches and regulations; as such, national supervisors may apply different criteria and rules for "overdue loans";
- Secondly, the amount of collateral on outstanding loans does not have to be compulsorily disclosed; IFRS does not gives any standard on how to assess the amount of collateral, and therefore practices vary a lot (from fair value to nominal value, to nominal realizable value and to "stressed" value) and that could potentially lead to severe inconsistencies;
- In many countries, the phenomenon of hiding NPLs exposures are pursued by building considerable amounts of restructured loans through the "evergreening" of the lending lines; the result is that bad debt exposures are not classified as such and the reported figures for NPLs actually underestimate the true situation of the banking system.

2.3 NPLs: A Booming Market

Whatever the definition and classification chosen, NPLs formation, in the aftermath of the global financial crisis, is currently a major trend in Continental Europe and elsewhere and a key phenomenon here to stay in the upcoming years and therefore worth of attention. This is suggested by a high level analysis of the key numbers of main European markets since the beginning of the financial crisis (see Fig. 2.1).

As seen in the graph above, the number of NPLs as a percentage of total gross loans in the European Union has more than doubled from the beginning of the global financial crisis in 2008 to-day. The trend is particularly relevant in some

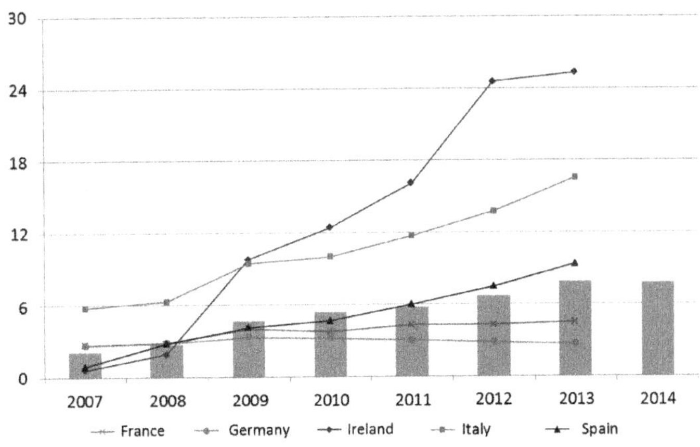

Fig. 2.1 NPL STOCK in the European Union. *Source* The World Bank Data (data.worldbank.org) and IMF Financial Situation Indicators

countries as Ireland, Spain and Italy, where the phenomenon has become a dangerous threat to the stability of the national financial systems. The upward trend in the amount of NPLs that started together with the outbreak of the global financial crisis in 2008 and steepened in the following years, was closely related to the economic cycle. A strong, yet unsustainable, economic boom pushed by high credit growth in the years 2003–2008 was followed by a period of deep recession (or very limited growth, with the notable exception of Germany). The abrupt end of the credit expansion cycle brought out many underlying problems, as the poor quality of many loans in the banks' balance sheets. Countries with an accentuated boom-bust cycle were considerably affected. The figures are particularly worrisome when we consider that the NPLs problem might have even been underestimated due to differences in accounting standards among countries, lack of data and underreporting of bad debt—as it is tipically the case in situations of top management continuity.

The upward trend in NPLs has relevant implications on the possibility of selling a portion of those bad loans, given the excess of supply over the sustainable demand for such assets. In any case, it appears that the overall stock of NPLs is likely to continue in the following years, since economic stress is not at an end yet. Also, the Asset Quality Review (AQR) conducted by the European Central Bank has led to capital shortfalls that will need to be covered, possibly by selling troubled risky assets—therefore contributing in the widening of the current gap between supply and demand. However, an increase in the percentage level and transparency of the coverage ratio should lower the current bid ask spread between the carrying value (book value on the banks' balance sheet) and market price, making sales more likelier to happen (as it gets easier to match demand and supply).

2.4 NPLs: A Macro and Micro Perspective

Given that the crisis was the determining force behind the upward trend in NPLs registered since 2008, we now take a closer look at the driving factors that were at work for the NPLs formation. In fact, from a theoretical standpoint, NPLs are affected by both macroeconomic factors and bank specific (microeconomic) factors.

In the first category—macroeconomic factors, the most relevant driver is probably GDP growth: a slowdown in the economy (and the connected higher unemployment rate) makes debt servicing harder and leads to an increase in NPLs. Also, the real estate cycle is critical, as a significant share of the banking loans are financing the acquisition of (and/or are backed by) real estate assets. Furthermore, strong interest rates play a relevant role, since their sudden and relevant increase makes repayment more expensive, especially in the case of floating rate loans. Higher inflation may results in a higher level of NPLs as well: debtors benefit from a reduction of the real value of the outstanding loan but, given that wages are usually sticky, this is compensated by a decrease of their real income, as measured at purchasing power parity. And excessive inflation may trigger central banks' reaction in the form of interest rates hikes. Exchange rate depreciation is then associated with an increase in NPLs. Finally, a higher risk aversion, as measured by the implied volatility indexes, leads to a rise in NPLs, because of the potential freeze on the banks' lending supply.

When looking at these factors, we realize that the main driver in the upward trend of NPLs of the last few years in continental Europe has certainly been the weak economic recovery. However, macroeconomic factors alone are insufficient to explain the variability in NPL ratios among different banks playing in the same regional market and with similar business models, and that is why it is useful to consider a second set of factors, related to bank specificities, can be helpful.

A first factor to be taken in consideration is capitalization: banks with a lower equity to assets ratio have an incentive to take on riskier projects, which can result in a moral hazard problem (as most of the risk is transferred to debtholders if things go badly). This means that on average the ratio of NPLs will increase for less capitalised institutions, a problem that is partially addressed thanks to higher and higher capital requirements. Also, excessive lending usually leads to the same outcome: less stringent controls over debtors result in more and more counterparties being unable to repay the loans and in a higher number of positions in arreas. A second aspect is that banks with a higher ROE are usually managed better and have more controls in place, which leads to fewer NPLs (and vice versa, lower NPLs ratio help in sustaining an above average ROE). It may seem a bit of a truism but, at the end of the day is very useful to remember that most severe credi quality problems are usually found in banks which are less profitable and less capitalised.

A last point to keep in mind, as already explained, is that differences in NPLs across countries have much to do with the different national regulatory frameworks. The fact that the increase of NPLs has been particularly pronounced in peripheral countries of the European market should not come as a surprise. On one side, those countries are the ones which are experiencing the slowest recovery. On the other side, they are also the places where the hardest legal hurdles are. Just as an example, the repossession of a collateral backing a retail mortgage can take many years in Italy, while it only lasts months in the United Kingdom or in Scandinavia (not to mention the United States).

2.5 NPLs: The Lake and the River

As seen, from a macroeconomic point of view the worsening of the overall economic and financial situation creates the conditions for an increase of the bad loans in the system. It is now necessary to highlight what is the lasting impact of this path to NPls accumulation on the financial system and its stability, not to mention its profitability and ability to create shareholders value.

When the amount of NPLs turns out to be progressively higher than expected, the balance sheet of banks deteriorate progressively, requiring write offs on stock loans and consequently lowering the bank's capital and dividend paying capacity.

Possibly, the bad debt problem could evolve into a threat for the liquidity and the solvency of the bank. The phenomenon is worsened by the fact that information asymmetries do not let investors distinguish between healthy and troubled assets. They tend therefore to ask, uniformly to all banks, and whatever their actual "true" financial situation, higher premia on the debt issued—therefore pushing down their stock price. More difficult and more expensive capital raisings then lead to reduced lending capacity. With lower credit available in the market, the number of defaulting counterparts tends to increase, together with the amount of bad loans in the balance sheets of banks, as in a self fulfilling profecy.

It is important to notice that bad debts not only create a "stock problem" (the lake progressively accumulating unhealthy loans), with the obvious implication that the regulatory capital of the bank tends to decrease because of the write offs on the NPLs that already sit on their Balance Sheet and because of the higher regulatory constraints posed by such a "weight". But also a "flow problem" (the river continuously filling the lake) develops through time, impairing significantly the income generating capabilities of the bank. The "flow problem" describes in fact a situation in which loans granted to a defaulting or defaulted party do not produce interest income anymore, while the bank still has to pay interests on its financial liabilities and all other kinds of operating costs. If the missed income from NPLs is not counterbalanced by the income from performing ones or from other activities, capital losses will occur from a Profit and Loss point of view. Moreover, the accumulation of non-performing loans will start impairing the banks' funding capacities, since the low rating and bad quality of its assets are neither making them ECB eligible for refinancing nor palatable for a possible sale unless a huge discount is applied to the bank's bonds price.

As previously analyzed, the way to hell is therefore large, smooth and quite busy (particularly in this last five–six years). Many are in fact the determinants of bad debt accumulation and numerous are the countries in Europe currently facing this challenge. The issue now is, given the current situation, how to get back to safety and profitability, getting the most out of past mistakes.

2.6 Ways Back from Hell

Past experiences from previous financial crisis show that the problem can rightfully be addressed and lasting recovery can be reached only if the amount of NPLs is progressively diminished back to a healthy level. In principle, NPLs can either be:

- Retained and managed by banks, who can work:
  - On their own. This approach requires having a sufficient set of knowledge and expertise in order to effectively tackle the issue. If the bank is not proficient enough, one risks leaving the problem as it is and letting it worsen through time;

  - Forming a joint venture or alliance with third parties, whilst retaining the majority and thus the lead in the governance of the work out unit. In this case, banks can team up with an institution with relevant capacities in dealing with a loan workout.

- Relocated or sold to one or more "bad banks", which can be:
  - Decentralized loan recovery companies, or Asset Management Companies (AMCs) that specialize in the management of impaired assets in order to unlock value;
  - A centralized AMC set up for public policy purposes (possibly when the size of NPLs reaches systemic proportion and no other way out strategy seems possible).

Action on NPLs can then be taken in or out of court. Often, banks have to go through an in-court enforcement of collateral which can take up to many years. In particular, countries with burdensome administrative procedures are particularly subject to the risk of low loans recovery, because of lengthy and not efficient judicial processes. Restructuring out of court takes shorter time and it is usually more cost-efficient. From the bank's point of view, better returns could be achieved through this procedure, by minimizing the delay and the cost of insolvency proceedings, by increasing the chances of a recovery of the debtor with his/her active support, and by a better flexibility in the managing tools. Still, out-of-court resolutions are quite underutilized. One of the reason could be found in the negative tax effects that debt write offs have and in the limited deductibility of provisions on bad debt, but also on the typical mind set of more traditional "work out units", which were born out of the Legal departments of the originating bank (and often filled with lawyers, with limited credit management and corporate finance experience).

One of the most common, yet totally ineffective, methods of dealing with NPLs is the already mentioned "evergreening" (or "extend and pretend"), that consists in refinancing both interest and principal payments so that the loan keeps being recorded as performing in the bank's balance sheet. Clearly, evergreening represents a way to set aside the problem without addressing it: no effort is made to diminish the stock of NPLs and no active recovery action is taken. The danger of this approach is to underestimate and ignore the problem, while it is actually growing and getting more and more critical. An alternative strategy, which consists in looking for quick profits in order to compensate for the flow losses, is clearly not going to turn into a lasting recovery pattern for the bank. This strategy could involve entering into riskier activities (when permitted by regulation) in order to balance the losses, dilute bad debts by increasing credit expansion (that, without a proper management for credit risk could result in further losses and in the ultimate default of the bank), or increasing the cost of newly issued loans (creating however a problem of adverse selection, since good and healthy customers are not prone to higher than market interest rates). As mentioned, all this kind of actions do not solve the emergency of NPLs since they do not take action on the root causes nor they try to pursue effective solution to empty the lake and stop the flowing of the river. If a bank chooses to handle the NPLs issue on its own, it therefore cannot do so by recurring to the borderline, unorthodox procedures mentioned above: an active approach in handling NPLs has to be designed and implemented in a timely way. The same is true if we consider the case in which a bank decides to cooperate with an external institution in order to manage its portfolios—also in this case the bank and the credit work out partner have to develop and execute a recovery strategy (or multiple recovery strategies) which is ensuring that large part of the value at risk will be collected.

2.7 The "Bad Bank" Approach

From a microeconomic perspective, mainstream academic literature suggests that it is possible to achieve value creation if a clean partition is operated and the troubled assets in a bank's balance sheet are separated from the healthy ones. Two categories of assets are then identified: on one side the NPLs, that will form the so called "bad bank", on the other side all the performing positions that will remain in the balance sheet of the "good bank". Economic value can then be created because of the optimal management of asymmetric information. As long as bad and good assets are mixed, investors cannot distinguish between a healthy and a troubled financial institution. Uncertainty about a bank's financial situation hampers its capacity to issue debt, lend, trade and raise additional capital. Creating a separate bank is therefore a successful expedient to communicate clearly to investors the high quality of the assets remaining in the good bank, whilst focusing the energy and attention of professional restructurers on the recovery activities associated with the bad bank. Value drivers other than the greater transparency created are in fact represented by the focalization of the skills and managerial talents of the management, supported by properly aligned incentives systems.

As simple as the idea is, in practice there are many organizational and structural aspects to be taken into careful consideration. Different features in the creation of a "bad bank" have to be considered and detailed since they can affect the bank's liquidity, solvency and overall profitability.

One option commonly considered is to proceed into a de-merger of the "bad bank". This model takes the characteristics of a spin-off or split-out of the equity shares, where the original bank takes the non-performing loans and (potentially) other risky assets (e.g. other sub performing loans and remaining non core activities). Some corresponding liabilities taken from the bank's balance sheet are also following those assets, as they all are de-merged into a legally separate banking entity. The new entity is then directly owned by the original "parent bank" (for the spin off option), or is directly owned by the current shareholders of the bank, which receives two shares (for the split out option)—one for the "bad bank" created by the demerging process, and one for the remaining "good bank". The transaction aims then to create value for the current shareholders, because they will retain the potential upside linked to the "bad bank" in case of a strong recovery in NPLs values.

Through the demerger, all the risks related to NPLs are in any case transferred along with the troubled assets to the new "bad bank" legal entity, thus improving the strategic flexibility and potential attractiveness to new investors of the remaining part of the original bank (the "good bank"). Moreover, the bank's capital could not be necessarily impacted by the write offs related to the NPLs as, on day one, the ownership of the assets is not changing anyway. However, this strategy presents some difficulties that are mainly connected to its timing and implementation costs. Spin-offs and spin-outs are complex operations and the set-up process is long and requires regulatory and legal qualifications (requires an extraordinary general meeting approval and regulatory authority). For all these reasons, even if effective, this approach is not commonly used.

The troubled financial institution could otherwise opt for the disposal and true sale of the "bad bank". In this case, all the non performing (and potentially, also the sub performing) lending assets are packed into an SPV (Special Purpose Vehicle) and then sold to one or more investors. The bad assets are taken off the balance sheet and this kind process has the benefit of being relatively fast, since no regulatory filing or special approval is required. Differently from the previous method, existing shareholders will not retain any benefit in case of an upside in the portfolio of NPLs.

In the case the bad bank is retained, banks could instead establish an internal restructuring unit, that focuses on managing in a specific and efficient way the troubled assets. This approach is taken in consideration mainly when the amount of unhealthy loans is a manageable, limited share of the total assets. In this case, the risk on the bad debt is not transferred outside the bank that still bears the consequences of a fluctuation in the value of NPLs and the possibility of further write-offs. However, proper and separate reporting on the activity of the internal restructuring unit can give a signal to the market of increasing transparency on the performance of the whole bank.

2.8 Systemic Bad Banks: The NAMA and SAREB Cases

Establishing a bad bank was the solution of choice of several European countries in the aftermath of the recent global financial crisis, in order to deal effectively with the system stability threatening risk connected with the increase in NPLs which followed the Lehman debacle.

As already mentioned, the extent of the NPLs phenomenon differed significantly among countries, with the so-called peripheral countries (or PIGS—Portugal, Ireland, Greece and Spain—with someone suggesting to add a further "I" for Italy) being the ones where the most significant increase took place. This explains why countries such as Germany had to take limited action, while in others the bad bank experience had a major impact. Among the PIGS countries, Ireland and Spain were the ones where the greatest amount of bad assets was disposed of, and hence a quick overview of their bad bank solutions will be provided.

In 2009 the National Asset Management Agency (NAMA), controlled by the National Treasury Management Agency, was established in Ireland in order to deal with the burst of the Irish property bubble. NAMA was set up as a bad bank: its purpose was to acquire illiquid property development loans (with an initial book value of €74 billions) from five Irish financial institutions through a SPV in return for government bonds. While the initially planned haircut on the book value was to be about 30 %, NAMA ended up acquiring the loans for €32 billion, at a 57 % discount. NAMA's situation was then compromised after 2010: the financial markets deemed the government support for banks excessive and this caused the yields on Irish bonds to rise. There were two main consequences. First, as the value of the assets in the "good banks" dropped, they were forced to raise more capital. Second, the ECB and the IMF were forced to bail out the Irish government itself with a €67 billions loan. Despite these facts, NAMA managed to perform well thanks to the major improvement in conditions in Irish commercial property market, and it aims now at recovering 80 % of loans by banks by 2016 (albeit at their nominal value, not discounted for the time value). As of today, while the NAMA bad bank seems in good shape, the Irish banking system is still facing difficulties, and the increase in NPLs is still going on. This shows that even setting up a national bad bank is not the ultimate solution to NPLs formation, because this approach relies on government support and it is highly sensitive to macroeconomic country specific factors and, most of all, even if it were able to address the NPLs stock issue cannot by itself stop the new flows one.

The bad bank set up in Spain was under many aspects similar to the one adopted in Ireland. In 2012 the Spanish government created an asset management company, referred to as SAREB, which started gathering troubled assets from financial institutions in order to allow them to manage the remaining "good bank" separately. The purchase was funded by government guaranteed bonds (which were zero risk weighted in order to reduce the capital burden) issued by SAREB. The assets purchased were mainly real estate backed loans: a portfolio of loans by 9 banks of €74 billions was at the end transferred to SAREB for €50 billion, with a 50 % average discount. As in the case of NAMA, both private investors (Spanish "healthy" banks) and the government (via its bank resolution vehicle, the FROB) provided the initial equity capital. SAREB is currently still fighting in order to become profitable, but overall it has contributed in handling a major part of the NPLs and in providing some relief to the Spain's troubled banking system, helping out and accelerating the consolidation of the sector and its restructuring and turn around.

Italy has been able to pride itself with being one of the few countries that survived the crisis without the need of a massive government intervention. The situation may come to an end as the country ponders the creation of a bad bank to deal with its massive NPL problem. According to the report published by ABI (Italian banker association) in January 2015, the gross value of "sofferenze", which are the NPLs subject of this book, had reached €181 billion. At the same time, the extent of distressed debt is in the range of €320 billion, at about 16 % of the total credit available in Italy. This explains why the creation of a bad bank, despite the great political controversies concerning it, seems if not the only, for sure one of the most effective ways out of this tricky situation. Additional measures are also being implemented in order to reduce the difficulties Italian banks are experiencing when trying to get rid of their NPLs. Specifically, the Italian government has worked to put in place legal reforms, aimed at speeding up the times required by the judicial system to allow the seizure of the collateral and at granting fiscal incentives, which should make write offs for banks if not easier at least more convenient from a cash flow and accounting point of view. In Fig. 2.2 is then described a potential approach in "breaking up" a troubled bank, by separating the bad and good bank components, with the critical role of the public intervention of the government in subscribing the equity piece of the bad bank (also funded by the good bank, but with more senior debt instruments), or offering some kind of public guarantee to private investors (see Fig. 2.2).

While the cases presented highlight how there is great potential in handling NPLs through the creation of a systemic bad bank, they also show that relying on government intervention alone cannot be considered a satisfactory solution. In fact, national institutions may be too slow in reacting at the evolution of possible problems; and in any case, current rules on "state aids" are becoming stricter and stricter, therefore preventing the intervention of the government if not in cases of extreme severity, as the notable Irish and Spanish examples are pointing out. In any case, it is worth to remember how "bad bank" is really a misnoumer, and often used with very different and sometimes confused means. It is actually safer to comment that there are in fact no such things as bad or good banks, but just bad or good "bankers" and "banking". This is why individual banks must take action in how

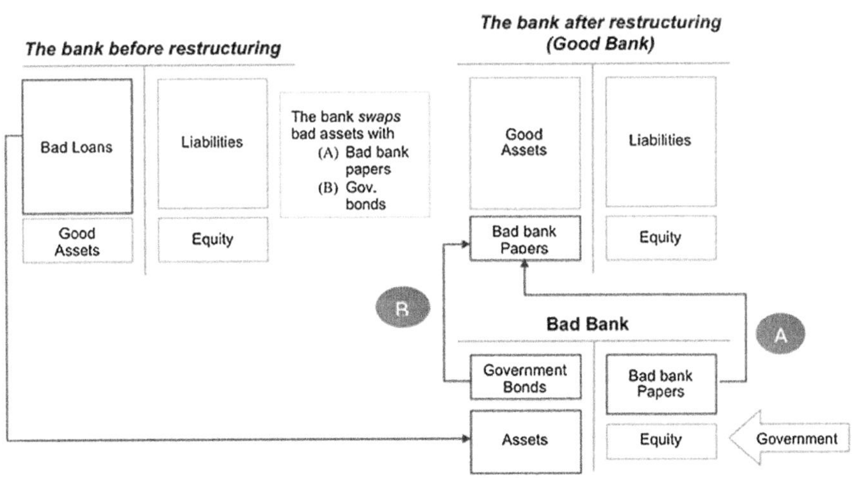

Fig. 2.2 A bad bank–good bank possible scheme. *Source* Bad Bank, Discussion Paper, Nomura —Investment Banking Financial Institution Group, 2009

they tackle the management of their NPLs with good bankers and good banking practices, as there is great value to be recovered from this difficult challenge. In doing that, good bankers will have not only to act fast and effectively—focusing on net present value and not just on the accounting view of the recovered value, but also they will have to do it in a holistic and active way, in order to fully achieve all the benefit a proper work out of their troubled credit assets can bring them.

Chapter 3
The Work-Out Value Chain: Permutations and Clusters

Abstract The credit work out activity should never be seen in isolation, but as a last, critical phase of a value chain that start with the origination and underwriting of loans. It follows that an optimal active management of non performing loans recovery and collection activities needs to be aimed for from inception. In this chapter, a quick overview and analysis of the main phases of the credit value chain is provided, with the purpose of identifying and highlighting the activities that need to be planned to ensure, at the end of the credit cycle and should things go wrong with the debtor, an optimal collection of the residual value. More specifically, an approach to the segmentation of the overall NPLs portfolio is provided, to definy homogeneous clusters, derived from all the possible permutations of relevant variable to consider, such as counterpart, size, nature of collateral etc.

Keywords Credit value chain · Credit workout · Active management · NPL portfolio segmentation · Strategies per NPL clusters · Make versus build · Independent workout platforms

3.1 The "Traditional" Credit Lifecycle

The previous chapter provided a definition of what a NPL is, but it did not explain how a loan that is initially performing could walk down the path that leads to become a non performing one. The first part of this chapter aims at fulfilling this purpose, by explaining how the entire credit lifecycle works and how loans transit from a phase of the cycle to the other. This analysis is also important because it emphasizes the fact that a loan naturally goes through multiple stages and that it is therefore essential to act across all of them in a consistent and seamless way, in order to avoid or at least minimize the probabilities of its deterioration. Rather than waiting for the problem to be apparent (and at that time, most likely in an irreversible way), banks must actively manage credits since the beginning, by carrying on the appropriate kind of proactive workout at each level of the life cycle.

C. Scardovi, *Holistic Active Management of Non-Performing Loans*,
DOI 10.1007/978-3-319-25363-3_3

Identifying critical symptoms and acting before the issue becomes incurable makes it possible to prevent the deterioration of many loans, focusing the credit work out management time only on those loans that are truly non performing and need therefore to be recovered at best, to minimize losses when the default finally happens.

3.1.1 Credit Origination

Each loan's history begins with the origination phase. A customer asks for a loan to a commercial or retail bank that, based on the determination of the risk profile of the counterpart, evaluates whether to grant her/him some credit line or not. At this stage, the bank collects data on the counterpart and on the commercial and financial set up of the loan—as publicly available or coming from specific analysis and interviews of the customer. All these information are relevant in order to asses the quality of the credit and the related risk adjusted pricing and may come handy also in case of a future default of the loan, to inform the most effective recovery actions available. Once all the relevant information has been gathered, the bank must determine the risk of the loans depending on their specific characteristics and estimate the associated expected loss. According to the regulatory rules introduced by the Basel II Accord, he bank may do so by choosing among three different approaches: standardized, foundation or advanced internal rating based (IRB). Depending on the choice adopted, the bank may need to set in place its own rating system, with specific estimates of the LGD (loss given default)—which are heavily dependent on the efficacy of the credit work out activities. Starting from the most simple approach, the standardized one, fixed risk weights are attributed to each loans category and scaled according to external credit ratings, so that no internal discretionary action is needed for their grading.

On the other hand, the remaining two approaches require a bank to determine some parameters in order to assess the counterparty risk. Under the foundation approach, a bank must estimate the probability of default of any single loan, which is the likelyhood that a debt will not be repaid in full in a certain time frame, usually one year. To determine such probability, the bank must analyze in statistically robust terms both quantitative and qualitative aspects of the credit risk of the counterparty. Such probability is then plugged into a formula, which is provided by the banking supervisor (the Central Bank of the country or region) together with the remaining relevant parameters, and the result of the final calculation determines the overall exposure and therefore the regulatory capital required to support the business (the higher the loans riskiness, the higher their expected loss and the higher the capital charges to the bank). Finally, the advanced internal rating based approach is the most sophisticated as it requires specific estimates not just for the probability of default (PD), but also of the exposure at the moment of default (EAD) and—more importantly—the loss in case of default (LGD or, in other complementary terms, the "cure rate" or "recovery rate" of the defaulted loan). The advanced approach calls for a lot of work from the risk management department, but its application usually results in lower capital requirements, and this is why most large institutions have adopted it. It is also important to note that the estimated parameters are subject to the review and approval of the supervisory authorities, and through them the bank determines the expected loss on the outstanding credits, which is given by the calculation of PD times EAD times LGD (times the maturity expressed in terms of years, as the basic formula estimates the expected losses for a one year time horizon). In any case, at the end of this process, the bank records the amount of the outstanding loans and the associated provisions, that should be linked to the expected losses—even if no deterministic rule is usually applicable and with significant variances registered amongst the banking players even if using the same techniques.

3.1.2 Credit Management

Once the credit has been originated, priced and rated (and a first generic, ex ante provision has been made), the next step is then managing the outstanding position. This involves updating information, monitoring the behavior and creditworthiness of the counterpart and running new analysis on the risk ratings in order to keep track of the status of the loan. This is vital because the evolution of the credit can take a multitude of possible patterns, and it is the bank's duty and in its direct interest to make sure that the one followed is the optimal one. It is usefull to reming that the monitoring and controlling activity of the bank is aimed at limiting any moral hazard incentive for the debtor—he/she could act in a very risky way, given that he/she would retain the full upside, whilst sharing most of the downside with the lenders. The monitoring and controlling activities of the bank are also providing—directly or indirectly—a number of useful information and renewed intelligence on the the health of the company, to the benefit of its multiple stakeholders and of the society at large.

3.1.3 Credit Management, Collection and Recovery

Depending on the development of the "health" of the loan itself, the final phase of the credit management lifecycle can either relate to its full collection (principal and interests) or to its partial recovery through active work out, in case the counterparty is defaulting. In a normal situation, most of the credits turn out to be performing and they are simply collected when their due date comes. But if an obligor fails to repay his debt within the contractual terms, the loan is considered past due and the counterparty may be subject to late fees and her/his rating status may be downgraded. This situation may be temporary and the borrower may promptly proceed in fulfilling his/her obligation within a short time frame, recovering in full his/her financial health, but if she/he fails to do so, the credit should be labeled as sub performing. Although there is no universal definition of what a sub performing loan is, it is clear that for this kind of credits it is unlikely that repayment will be completed just through the standard collection of principal and interest: the bank may need to restructure the debt in order to help out the debtor's financial stabilization and make therefore repayments possible, even if at different terms or over a longer period of time. Hopefully, most of the restructured loans may be brought back to a performing status, even if—usually—at the expense of the overall profitability of the loan.

In case the restructuring is not successful, the last stadium of the deterioration is reached when the loan becomes non performing. As explained in the previous chapter, the convention—and the general rule introduced by the Basle II Accord—is to mark this transition when the debt becomes past due for over 90 days, but generally speaking, the category may sometimes refer to any loan that will not be repaid in full or that has been restructured. In case the loan is definitely becoming non performing, a final phase entails the start of a formal recovery process, which could involve the sale of the collateral and other judicial or extra judicial process—the optimal credit recovery being the main focus and ultimate target of the WHAM approach that will be further discussed in the next chapters.

3.2 A More Proactive Approach to the Credit Lifecycle

As described, as the loan goes through many different phases, a bank may choose to adopt a more active and holistic approach to minimize the potential losses, e.g. to maximize the recovery value should anything go wrong with the lending facility. In fact, credit workout should not be interpreted as the "ambulance chasing", e.g. as an extraordinary approach to manage emergency situations. As it is quite normal and unavoidable to expect some of the loans to turn sour in due time, the bank must act across all phases of the credit lifecycle—from the origination to its final collection or recovery—as to maximize its embedded capacity to manage sub or non performing situations.

3.2.1 Credit Origination

As pointed out many times in the previous chapter, for a bank being excessively lax in the concession of credit is an easy way for increasing the interest margin in the short run, but also an even surer way to get into serious trouble in the medium term—building a huge stock of distressed debts that could bring the bank to the technical default stage (with regulatory capital below the minimum regulatory requirements) or even to its ultimate bankruptcy. This is why the first phase, the one of credit origination, is critical. Even at this early stage a bank should adopt a "what if things go wrong" mindset, developing a framework that could help it manage the loan and maximize its cure rate in case of deterioration, creating a good reliable database to use at later stages and ensuring that the overall collateral is correctly valued, monitored, repossed (if needed as this turns out to be the best recovery strategy) and, finally, sold to a third counterparty in order to maximize the cash returned to the bank—taking into account the related collection costs and the time value of money (the longer the time required to collect the money, the lower its present value).

A correct management of this phase involves therefore getting information efficiently (in a short time frame and with low operating costs) and effectively (verifying that it is accurate and up to date) about both the debtor and the specific contractual structure of the loan. For what concerns the debtor, a bank must gather accurate data about his basic record (such as a client's bank code, city of residence, the work activity, the payment history) and legal information (the Court in charge, any legal procedure undergoing, the typology of any legal action and the legal action status). To this end, a bank aiming at building a comprehensive database to use for recovery and credit collection, may want to add other kind of information. These could possibly have a more industrial nature and with more specific reference to the underlying collateral, especially in the case of corporate loans financing a specific project or for real estate development financing (as discussed in later chapters).

A greater extent of analysis is then required for any kind of valuation, as one must not simply report the asset's basic information, but also gauge, for example, how much a collateral could be worth under a fire sale scenario, taking into account the prevailing market situation (average price, transaction average time) and the possible additional costs (taxes, insurance, maintenance etc.) the bank may have to face in order to properly sale the asset and recover as much cash as possible. Origination is hence not a trivial step, and this is why it is worthwhile to do it in the best possible way, gathering all the data and intelligence that could support its effective workout if required.

3.2.2 Credit Management

Once the loan is on the bank's book, it must be properly managed. Firstly, this means making sure that all the information kept on record is up to date. Secondly, it means tracking all the changes of the variables which may determine the evolution of performing loans into sub or nonperforming loans. There are several critical thresholds to monitor and manage actively from one stage to the other, and identifying them is not an easy task. In fact, despite the fact that for some of them there is a regulatory definition, this is just partially helpful as their economic meaning is what really matters in assessing the risk of transition of a loan from one stage to another. This is why each bank should establish a set of early warning signals (EWS), that may act as a ringing bell (or lead indicators) and allow the determination, as soon as possible, of any possible deterioration in the credit quality. EWS must of course be statistically significant and limited in number, in order to make their monitoring feasible and pragmatically manageable and actionable.

3.2.3 Active Management of Sub Performing Loans

Once the bank identifies the loans that show some initial critical issues, e.g. the sub performing ones, it must assess whether they are large enough to cover the costs of implementing corrective actions (or viceversa, it should just let them go, stopping short of any direct or indirect action and hoping they will recover and get back to full performing). If the possible benefits coming from these actions exceed the efforts and the related costs it must undertake, the bank should proceed further and prioritize the most urgent and relevant issues and take appropriate corrective steps. These actiones can take different forms, but it is important to notice that at this stage they are still in the realm of moral suasion, because the obligor has not yet defaulted, and therefore the bank has no control over the collateral, nor it can enforce any legal action to seize it. Nevertheless, an active management of the sub performing loans requires the implementation of some measures to address the situation well in advance the clear and, at that time, almost certainly not revertable manifestation of the non performing state of the loan.

On one side, a number of financial actions can be taken so that to minimize the exposure at the time of the potential, future default; on the other side, industrial actions can reduce the chances of the borrower defaulting, by enabling and supporting the counterpart in completing the appropriate managerial actions (e.g. executing a well defined restructuring plan, usually involving cost cutting) that will allow him/her to repay the debt in full. Of course, this kind of actions may require the assistance of restructuring specialists—hired and working for the debtor who is still in full control of the company/asset being financed by the bank. In fact, these actions can only be carried out if the debtor decides of his/her own free will to support and execute the restructuring plan suggested by the advisor. If, despite all the measures taken, the loan moves into the non performing state, an active recovery strategy is then needed—e.g. the focus shifts from the minimization of the probability of default and of the exposure at default to the minimization of the loss given default (or, said in another way, the maximization of the cure or recovery rate on the troubled loan).

Once the loan reaches the non performing status, the bank approach may then switch from moral suasion to direct action: the bank could decide to keep managing the relation with the debtor through extrajudicial procedures and processes or, viceversa, can proceed taking legal action against the debtor. In any case, it must keep acting proactively and use its full set of capabilities to extract the highest value it can. Figure 3.1 summarizes the different steps of the lifecycle of a bank loans and associates to each of them both the normal basic procedures and the more proactive

	Origination	Management	Collection/Recovery
Basic operations	• Collect obligor and loan data • Determine credit risk - develop rating models - compute PD, EAD, LGD • Estimate expected loss	• Monitor and manage risk rating • Update information • Run back-testing of ratings	• Collect performing credits • Evaluate options for sub-performing loans • Enforce legal actions for non-performing loans
Workout strategy	Build a database that can be used in case recovery is needed: - collect also information of industrial nature - evaluate collateral under a sale perspective	• Establish a set of Early Warning Signs (EWS) • Monitor EWS and report loans that break thresholds	• Sub-performing loans: moral suasion - financial actions - industrial actions • Non-performing loans: direct action

Fig. 3.1 Credit lifecycle and active credit management

workout strategy that could be implemented and that will be further detailed later on.

The next section will then focus on how to best approach the recovery process once the loan granted by the bank is assessed to be non performing. Indeed, several "holistic" aspects must be taken in consideration in order to deal with the distressed situation and in the most efficient and effective way as possible, taking into consideration the speed of the entire process.

3.2.4 Active Management of Non Performing Loans

As already mentioned, acting proactively on the loan throughout its lifecycle in order to prevent and minimize the chances it will become a troubled asset. Notwithstanding, when its situation turns to the worst, the debtor defaults and the loan is then definitely classified as non performing. At this point in time the workout process becomes critical and the only way to get some of the money back. At this stage, since the possibility of its recovery to a performing status is pretty much zero, the bank has to plan and execute its work out activities in order to try to recover as much value as possible from the loan—addressing all the guarantees it may have, starting from any "hard" collateral attached to the loan, such as a real estate or an equipment tangible asset. While in the previous phases of the credit life cycle the bank usually exercises just some "soft" moral suasion on the borrower, when the loans become non performing some direct action could and should be taken, as the bank can now act towards the debtor both in a judicial and extrajudicial way and it can operate on the collateral as well, seizing it to become its direct owner.

In doing this, a bank can decide to manage the non performing loan through its internal division of credit recovery, the so called "captive" work out solution (further detailed in later chapters). As an alternative, the "non captive" approach can consider the externalization of this task to third party servicers, that are usually highly specialized entities already operating in the open market and that are able to exploit economies of scale and a focused and unbiased approach to the collection of the credit (as pure players, the independent work out platforms do not have the potential conflicts of interest a bank may have, given that this last one continues to have multiple commercial relationships either with the defaulted debtor or with its affiliates and stakeholders—e.g. the entrepreneur of a defaulted SME may well still remain a private and wealthy client of the bank!).

The choice of staying "captive" or going "extra captive"—usually not a black and white one, as multiple mixed set ups could be identified, is based on a strategic assessment of the bank's internal capabilities, but it is also driven by the phase of the economic cycle, as in periods of deep recession banks may end up owning such large amounts of NPLs that they cannot efficiently manage them all, and are therefore forced to outsource at least part of them to deal with the extra volume.

Whether captive or not, the main question entails the "how to" properly act on the portfolio of non performing loans to maximize their recovery value. As it could be expected, there is no single approach able to fit all kind of situations, but each non performing loan should be evaluated under a well developed framework to determine what the optimal solution could be. An undifferentiated and unfocussed management of a NPLs portfolio would have a negative effect on the workout process because it would lack both efficiency and effectiveness. Operative and managing cost would have a high impact if each credit, especially if small, was handled separately without considering the share of the activities that could be pooled together to share economies of scale.

Viceversa, the undifferentiated pool of unrelated activities could not realize relevant economies of scale, whilst at the same time hindering significantly the effectiveness of the recovery process.

Moreover, during pick times, following long phases of economic recession, a very large amount of non performing loans in the banks' balance sheets would in any case saturate the operative capacity to handle it, creating further volatility in the efficacy and effectiveness of the recovery strategy (the cost structure would rapidly become very costly and suboptimal, and the effectiveness of the recovery would further deteriorate).

3.3 Segmentation of Non Performing Loans

To better define what a differentiating and focussed approach to credit work out and collection would look like, it is important to consider whether the overall loans portfolio is made up of plain lending (e.g. "banking book") or leasing (e.g. "leasing book"), or a balanced mix of both. In fact, in the case of leasing, the bank is the direct owner of the underlying good being financed (whether the good is a real estate, an equipment, a car/boat/plane etc.). The bank therefore bears most of the burdens and potential risks—not just financial, but also tied to potential liabilities that could come from any direct or indirect damage created by the good itself—with further potential losses and reputational issues to be considered. Instead, for all the remaining loans, the bank does not have the property of the asset being financed, and could only end up being its owner in case it will need to take possession of the collateral to recover some of the outstanding value of the NPL.

Once a first segmentation between the banking and leasing books has been done, further segmentational criteria could be introduced, to further clusters the NPL portfolios. In our experience and typical working hypothesis, the main segmentational drivers for further clustering the banking business are kind of counterpart, ticket size, vintage, presence of a third party guarantee and kind of collateral. Within each cluster, a further segmentation is designed to create smaller buckets and to identify even more specific kinds of defaulted debt. For what concerns the size of the files, NPLs are generally subdivided in four sections, generally identifying loans of value up to 25,000€, 100,000€, 500,000€ and 5,000,000€. The higher the value of the loan, the more critical and worthy of attention it will be for the bank work out activities. However, banks usually hold as asset a sizable amount of small loans, whose single positions would be individually difficult to manage, but that overall could represent an important share of the bank's non performing exposures and could be effectively managed as an aggregate position.

When clustered on the basis of age or vintage, NPLs are generally divided among loans that have been defaulted for more than two years, from two to seven years or more than seven years. The younger the NPLs, the higher the probability that their exposure will be recovered at least partially. Therefore, banks will have to act more aggressively and speedily and—given the current stock at hand, prioritize the most recent loans. It is important to underline that vintage is usually referred to the origination month. Partitioning portfolios according to this criteria allows then to check for the correlation between a given risk factor and the time of the issue of the loan. Vintage analysis has in fact relevant implications. It is a useful tool for monitoring a portfolio's current risk level and for comparing risk levels at particular points in time. It allows to define connections between a particular characteristic and credit risk; and in a dynamic perspective it enables to forecast risk levels in the future and to verify whether risk policy changes have had a positive influence on the portfolio's risk. For example, it allows to study the evolution of cumulative losses through time, and to verify whether there is a connection between losses reported and practices put in place by a bank following a certain period of time.

The presence of the collateral gives then the bank the option to actively act on it in order to retrieve at least a significant part of the outstanding loans. According to the nature of the collateral, loans can be segmented into homogeneous buckets and the underlying asset is priced at market values through the analysis of its initial cost, obsolescence, ease of sale and historical prices for sales of similar goods. In the case of the banking book, the collateral is usually a real estate asset, therefore the bank has to determine an optimal way to manage it and to bring this to the market. For this active management of the underlying real estate asset, there are many options and "smart" approaches that could be taken in consideration and that will be analyzed in the following chapters.

Finally the fourth cluster is subdivided between loans that have or have not initiated a judicial procedure—with very different impacts given the Country specific typical throughput time and effectiveness of judicial procedures.

3.4 Permutations and Clustering of NPL Portfolios

Given the segmentational approach introduced in the previous paragraph for the baking book, we could classify and identify up to 48 different clusters—given the possible number of permutations that could be mathematically derived (see Fig. 3.2). Among the different segmentational criteria, we would still suggest to consider as the main focus the credit size and the age/vintage, in order to optimize the "make" or "buy" strategy (the level of outsourcing in the management of the NPLs the bank may choose to follow). Similarly to the banking book, we could proceed on the leasing one, where usually three main segmentational criteria are identified. The segmentation according to the size of the file is identical to the case of a banking position, while the aging usually distinguishes only between contracts that are younger or older than two years. Even more important than for the banking book, type and nature of the collateral should be considered (technically, the asset related to a leasing contract is not even a "collateral", as it is bought and owned by

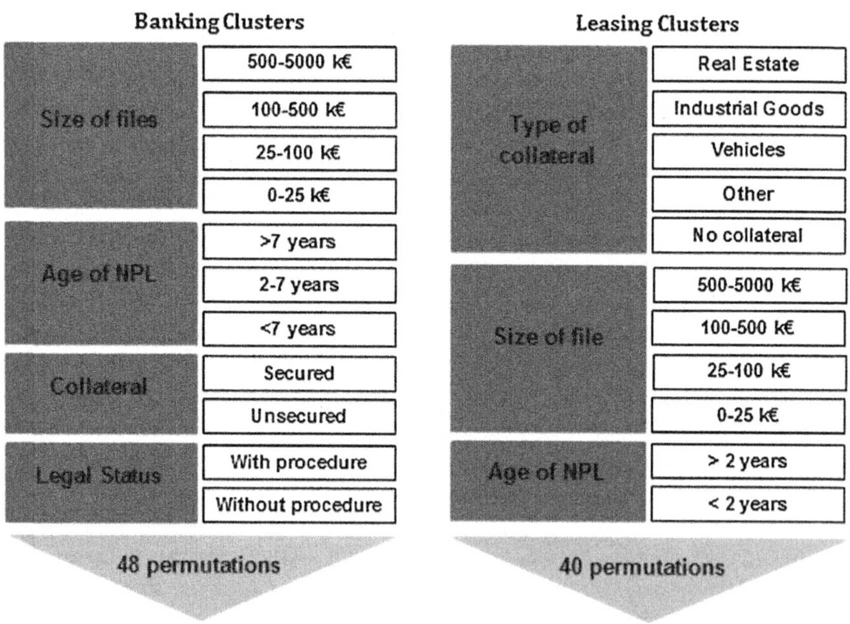

Fig. 3.2 Segmentation of an NPLs portfolio. Example of clusterization of banking and leasing positions. *Source* AlixPartners

the bank, with the client of the bank repaying the leasing contract associated with the use of the good, given the time horizon that has been contractually defined).

As mentioned, the kind of assets that can be associated to a leasing contract are various: they could be real estate assets, equipment/industrial goods, cars/boats/planes, but also infrastructure (e.g. renewable energy plants), or even furniture. The extreme variability of the collateral is therefore critical for the bank, since it could consist in an asset that has no active secondary market and therefore it is difficult to value and sell—it could in fact has been developed for the specific uses of the lessee and could need specific, technical knowledge to be managed, operated and remarketed. Even in the case of a more standard kind of good, it could however loose value quickly over time—because of technical obsolescence, malfunctioning issues etc. For the leasing book, given the level of segmentational criteria adoptable, and the number of permutations that could mathematically follow, the number of possible clusters amount to 40, with a greater focus given, as already mentioned, to the nature of the asset at the center of the leasing contract, in order to identify the "industrial know-how" required for an optimal process of work out and value recovery.

Figure 3.2 summarizes, for the banking and leasing books, the categorization of loans into segments and the potential clusters attainable through their mathematical permutation—we suggest that any bank, or independent credit work out unit, should define in a hydiosincratic way the number of segmentational criteria and therefore target clusters on the basis of their overall credit recovery strategy, sophistication, level of ambition and—of course—current stock of NPL portfolios. The clusters shown above are just a way to handle the situation; potentially different clusters can be chosen to categorize different portfolios and for different kind of banks or independent credit work out platforms.

3.5 Credit Work Out Strategies for NPL Clusters

Given a high level of sophistication and ambition, the number of possible permutations and therefore NPLs clusters could easily get to a few hundreds, even if a 20–30 of them can explain most of the work out activities being carried out. For any of these permutations—e.g. defined NPL clusters, a detailed analysis of the best specific strategies to recovery and of the smartest ways to build consistent capabilities to realize those recoveries should be carried out.

For each NPL cluster, the bank should start determining the gross book value (GBV) in order to quantify the total volumes to be managed (both in terms of GBV and number of positions). The bank should also start assessing whether a judicial or an extra judicial strategy will be most likely pursued, as this kind of decisions are heavily influencing the overall effort expected and the strategic decision on the potential full or partial outsourcing of the activities that will need to be performed. Based on this initial hypothesis, the bank can also start planning the required men days for the work effort required, and the expected cash flow attainable by year and for each cluster.

An overall target rate of recovery that the bank rationally expects to be able to achieve should also be assigned to each NPL cluster. This target rate of recovery for any of the cluster depends of course on the characteristics of the debt itself: a higher recovery rate should be expected for a more recent, and more collateralized loan. The recovery rate is usually expressed as a percentage of the gross book value and in nominal terms as well. However, a more useful target should consider the time value of the money recovered, e.g. comparing the net present value of all the future cash-in (net of the costs incurred) and the original GBV of the NPL. It is therefore important not to rely exclusively on purely nominal recovery targets as these could create potential arbitrage opportunities and a significant misalignment in the incentives of the managers leading the work out and recovery efforts. In fact, we could even state that, assuming some level of inflation and a collateral whose real value is somehow resilient through time (e.g. a real estate asset), there is always some kind of holding period that allows the full recovery of the GBV—the work out manager just need to be patient, and without doing anything at all… just letting time pass and inflation doing its work on the market (nominal) value of the collateral!

But should the bank's shareholders really be happy and reward the credit work out manager that is able to recover the entire nominal value of the GBV of an NPL real estate backed in 40 years, with an average inflation through this time horizon of 4–5 %? Doing the proper math, we would find out that the net present value of that collection is almost zero! And net present value is what really matters—as it correctly focuses on net cash flows and taking into consideration their timing and the purchasing power of the money recovered at all the different points in time. For this very reason, if the bank is using one or more external credit work out platforms, it should calculate the success fees awarded to the counterparts as a percentage of the recovery rate realized as a net present value—and not in nominal terms as it still happens in most of the market situations as of today.

Summing up, for each NPL cluster it is necessary to determine the best strategy to recovery that maximizes the net present value for the shareholders of the bank. One critical decision entails the choice of the process to e pursued and that could be judicial, extrajudicial or mixed, and the level of outsourcing that will be pursued. In any case, whether the management of the NPL cluster will be retained internally or not, the bank needs to quantify the volumes managed in terms of gross book value and number of positions, but also in terms of targeted rate of recovery—expressed both in nominal and in net present value terms—and the success fees associated with that, in case it will select some level of outsourcing (or just to correctly incentivize its work out management team, in case it decides to do all the work internally).

3.6 Economics of the Recovery Strategies and "Make" Versus "Build"

For each NPL cluster, once the recovery targets are defined, the bank has to determine the related economics for the each of the selected recovery strategies. There are a certain amount of costs associated to the workout of each NPL cluster. Those costs can be both fixed and variable, determining a different operating leverage (the higher the fixed component, the higher the operating leverage). If managed internally, fixed costs are usually higher, as it will be the operating leverage: usually, they include the bank's personnel that will actively work on the loans to recover as much as possible, and the costs related to the operations and to the technology owned by the bank for that purpose. However, a high operating leverage could be risky for the bank, because it would be more sensible to shifts in the volume of NPLs, also potentially influencing the expected performance, and most importantly, the actual recovery rate on those loans. On the other hand, outsourcing would require the bank to pay a variable fee (usually structured as a flat retainer, plus some level of success fees driven by the actual recovery), that is relatively higher than the internal cost, but it is variable and depends on the number of loans outsourced and by the performance attained by the third party platform (therefore, strongly incentivizing the counterparts—usually more, as the bank's internal incentive systems are usually quite limited and capped).

Given the recovery strategy being pursued, and considering the critical relevance played by the cost structure of the activities required, the bank has to determine the right capabilities and mix of fixed versus variable costs through which it can optimally manage its portfolios of NPLs. It is easier, for example—at least in the short run, to manage a big ticket loan internally because the high expected recovery rate can justify the high fixed costs associated with it. On the other hand, if the bank holds a portfolio with an important overall size of small loans, the right decision could be to manage them externally: the lower amount recovered on each loan of the portfolio may not be enough to justify the costs of setting up an internally managed and highly industrialized recovery procedure, and the higher variable fees on the outsourcing could still leave some net recovery margin for the bank.

Usually the banks, having to deal with a number of heterogeneous portfolios of NPLs, with different sizes, maturities and characteristics, decide for a mix of both "make" and "buy" strategies.

In the case of the "make" strategy, e.g. pursuing the full internalization of the credit work out activities, the bank has to determine the best allocation of workloads for different internal profiles—senior and junior employees and managers. The internal effort from a human resources side needs to be carefully assessed, as this cost component will weight heavily on the overall cost structure, and—needless to say—the quality of the people employed (and their incentive system) will play a crucial role on the expected recovery performance of the work out unit, and in a different way for each of the NPL clusters already defined (e.g. more critical files will need better talents and could justify, in economic terms, their higher employment costs).

In the case of a "buy" strategy, the calculation of expected external fees will be sufficient to determine the overall economics, but a detailed comparative analysis of a number of third party outsourcing solutions available should be evaluated vis a vis the expected recovery rate that could be associated to the different platforms. When the expected recovery rate ends up as being in any case too low compared to the costs associated to it, the bank can decide to sell the portfolio of NPLs to third parties, e.g. financial sponsors specializing in high risk/high return credit investments. Another possible solution is to seek alliances with other banks, sharing the internal resources and mixing them with new ones joining from the market to develop a better credit work out platform—clubbing the skills and pooling the volumes. This could be a valuable idea for small or medium banks that need to reach a critical mass of NPLs to be able to set up a credible credit work out—or just to have the required credibility to execute a major competitive sale of NPLs in the market.

Once the positive and negative sides of internally managing the recovery of NPLs versus outsourcing are determined, it is important to establish some criteria to support the bank in the decision on how much it should go for each solution. Theoretically, the bank should try to outsource as much as possible: as already mentioned, this would allow it to diminish fixed costs and therefore to be less exposed to the operational risk driven by a highly inflexible cost structure. However, the decision is not so easy, since there is a substantial trade off between the fees asked as compensation by a third party provider and the effective extra recovery that the bank can hope for from the adoption of the outsourced credit recovery strategy.

3.7 Cost Income Analysis for Independent Work Out Platforms

For independent credit work out platforms, the analysis of the economics attainable for each of the NPL clusters defined must include a Profit and Loss analysis—in fact, the final scope of this companies is to generate for them an interesting and sustainable net income as they are, de facto, advisory platforms selling their know how and active management capabilities to banks—a unique mix of consulting companies and asset managers in the best cases. More specifically, the analysis of the economics for an independent credit work out unit is heavily weighted on the analysis of the cost income of the associated servicing mandates negotiated with the different banks which are clients to the platform. The credit work out unit has therefore to estimate the expected revenues by year in terms of cash flows, in turn considering different levels of outsourcing across the value chain and for each specific NPL cluster being defined and served. In a parallel way, costs must also be estimated by year and nature, internal—as personnel, IT, and support functions—and external—for outsourcing, legal fees, data and information required etc. For this kind of analysis, some key performance indicators can be useful to assess the profitability and productivity of the independent credit work out unit. Example of such key indicators are ratios as such the "cost to income", the "revenues by employee", the "total recovery (nominal or—much more correctly—as net present value) per gross book value", the "total fees per unit of recovery" etc.

By analyzing the profit and loss associated with each portfolio being served, the independent credit work out unit has to assess whether and what kind of recovery activity is worth (or not at all) for each NPL cluster. For specific NPL portfolios, if the recovery rate is very low and the costs incurred for the (rather desperate) tentative of recovery are comparably much higher, the credit work out unit would be better off just winding down these portfolios. However, a trade off would also arise, for the independent credit work out (being paid for not doing anything is not an attractive proposition to potential clients) and for the client banks (if there is the perception that for some credit no recovery action will be taken anyway, the debtors would be incentivized to default even more and quite freely—given the limited consequences they could expect).

Ultimately, the choice will be taken to optimize a trade off that would consider wasting resources in a non recoverable position on one side and giving to the market a negative signal on the other, since winding down NPLs without any recovery effort at all would create a chain effect based on the "moral hazard" playing in favour of the debtors. In an hypothetical case study, we performed a scenario analysis in order to determine the most efficient mix of outsourcing and recovery rate that would allow a credit work out platform to minimize its cost income (given that most part of the income is driven by the success fees paid by the client banks on the basis of the actual recovery rate), but also taking into consideration such kind of "side effects" and potential distorsions. In any case, the scenario analysis should be performed separately for the banking and leasing portfolios, since they show very different recovery rates and associated costs. On one side, it should consider multiple potential scenarios impacting on the estimated recovery rate and on the related revenues: e.g. considering a minimum, average and maximum recovery rate. On the other side, multiple scenarios should also be considered to determine how much to push on the outsourcing lever: e.g. high, basic, low or no outsourcing at all.

What is usually emerging from this kind of analysis is that no outsourcing at all would lead to the worst case scenario for both banking and leasing portfolios. As for a credit work unit internal to the bank, also for most of the independent credit

Cost Income Scenario Analysis

BANKING

Outsourcing Level	Recovery Rate: MIN	Recovery Rate: AVERAGE	Recovery Rate: MAX
HIGH	>90%	>80%	>80%
BASIC	>80%	>80%	>70%
LOW	>90%	>80%	>80%
NONE	>100%	>100%	>100%

LEASING

Outsourcing Level	Recovery Rate: MIN	Recovery Rate: AVERAGE	Recovery Rate: MAX
HIGH	>90%	>90%	>90%
BASIC	>90%	>80%	>80%
LOW	>100%	>90%	>90%
NONE	>100%	>100%	>90%

Fig. 3.3 Cost income scenario analysis for credit work out. Cost income scenario analysis performed separately for banking and leasing. *Source* AlixPartners

work out platforms it is true that they are not sufficient by themselves to support an efficient management of the different credit recovery strategies, not only because the volume of NPLs is too high to be properly handled but also because revenues are not sufficient to compensate for the costs required, which are mainly fixed. The best combinations are therefore usually found when the expected recovery rate is at a maximum or average level—e.g. the platform is focusing on the NPL clusters for which it really has some competitive advantage in the effectiveness of credit recovery—and the level of outsourcing is from low to high—e.g. the platform decides on the "make" versus "buy" strategies on the basis of the credit characteristics as defined for each cluster (see Fig. 3.3).

In the example below (see Fig. 3.4), the red dotted line highlights the best scenario combinations for the independent credit work out unit, which imply at

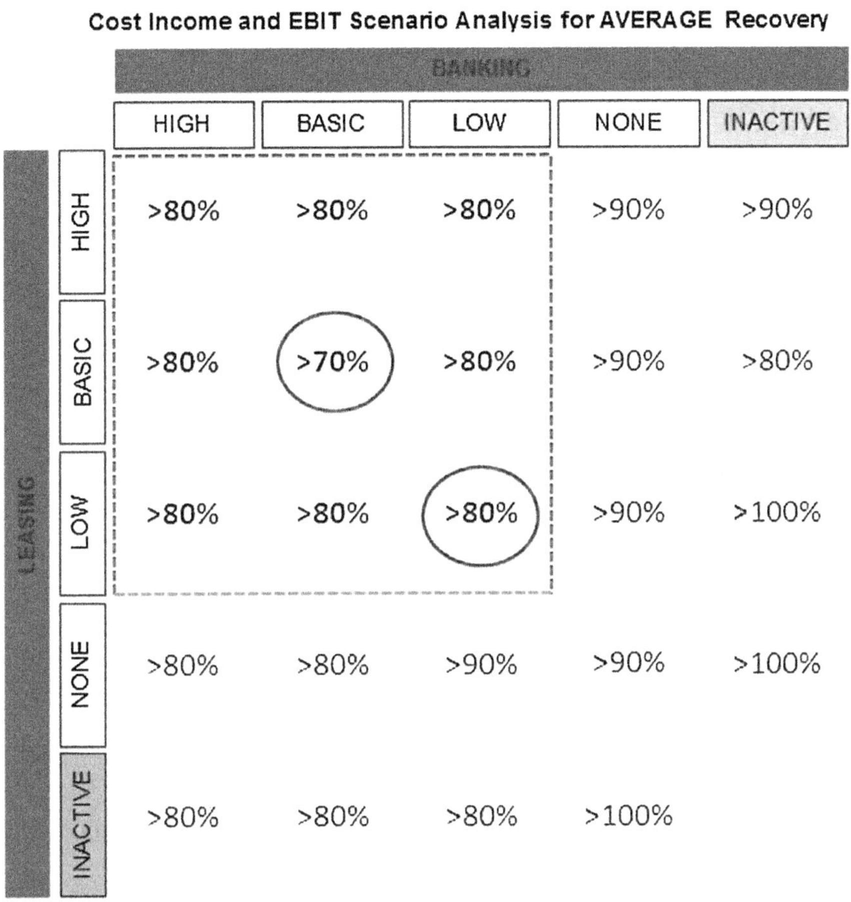

Fig. 3.4 Cost income scenario analysis for credit work out. Cost income scenario analysis performed for banking and leasing at the same time. *Source* AlixPartners

least a minimum level of outsourcing. The circled cost/income ratios represent instead the boundaries of such best scenarios range. The bottom boundary corresponding with the better off scenario is the basic level of outsourcing, while the upper boundary is the low level of outsourcing—also based on an EBIT scenario analysis.

Chapter 4
The Work-Out Unit: Captive–Deceptive

Abstract The proper governance of the credit work out activities is a key element to maximize the recovery value of a NPLs portfolio. Credit work out could in fact be carried out internally and be seamlessly embedded in the organization, or carried out by third parties; a number of other intermediate solutions could also be defined and executed. A "captive" work out unit has some advantages in terms of work simplification and coordination with the remaining parts of the bank. But a non captive is usually more efficient in ensuring the best alignment of incentives and a performance comparable with the market best practices. Eventually, a properly set up internal work out unit could be segregated, developed through external partnerships and "brought to market", e.g. competing to get further NPLs to manage and become a fee generating, profit seeking business.

Keywords Credit workout governance · Recovery maximization · Captive workout unit · Non-captive workout unit

In the previous chapter, we have pointed out that there is no single strategy for the optimal management of NPLs, and that several factors have to be taken into consideration when deciding what the best approach to adopt could be. We also pointed out that a particularly critical point for each bank is identifying the optimal level of externalization for its workout operations, which involves taking into account that different classes of loans require different treatments as their reaction to similar factors may not be identical (and that there could be issues of overall maximum capacity too). Even once the bank has managed these complexities and decided the proper degree of outsourcing, there still are multiple strategic and operational options to consider.

This chapter aims at providing a comprehensive list of the possible, alternative credit management set ups, highlighting the pros and cons connected with each of them. This kind of framework should therefore help banks in identifying the best solution for the development and management of a credit work out unit of excellence.

The choice is crucial, because it has a tremendous impact on the way NPLs are handled: different set ups may lead the bank to overweight the importance of

C. Scardovi, *Holistic Active Management of Non-Performing Loans*,
DOI 10.1007/978-3-319-25363-3_4

achieving maximum recovery (the dream of a CLO—Chief Lending Officer) versus other objectives, such as the cost optimization of the platform itself (the main aim of the COO—Chief Operating Officer). Each of these decisions leads to a trade-off between conflicting goals, and these must be managed in order to strike an optimal balance. Firstly, while some level of conflict among different targets is inevitable, its extent must be reduced. Secondly, a bank must be aware that different set ups may lead to different credit management patterns—which may be differently (more or less) suited for the diverse phases of the economic cycle. These must also be monitored in order to align the incentives that each of the options creates to the overall goals of the bank, including its lending commercial strategy.

4.1 Alternative Set Ups: Captive Versus Non Captive

At a first level, the degree of externalization of the workout process determines whether a bank will need to structure its own "fully loaded" workout unit or will just be able to rely mostly on external servicers. Outsourcing may be desirable because the existence of multiple players in the market creates competition among them and leads to greater efficiency and (potentially) transparency. It could also—and rather obviously—lead to a more flexible cost structure, characterized by a lower operating leverage. This is particularly true when we consider that several servicers are paid a low fixed or "base" fee (retainer), and then make most of their profits through the variable fee, which depends on their performance in terms of the overall amount recovered (success fee). Increasing the volumes allocated to the same external servicers also allows them to achieve economies of scale, further reducing their costs per unit of production. Besides fostering efficiency, outsourcing has benefits also in terms of better transparency: NPLs are managed in an open marketplace with significant components of success fees that help in progressively revealing their actual value. This increases confidence among market participants and therefore the appetite of potential financial investors. It may thus reduce the haircuts which they would otherwise be applying to less transparent loans, leading to transactions that are closer to their fair value.

Despite the above mentioned advantages and the centrality of the credit work out activities carried out by external suppliers in the recovery process, most of the universal banks still rely only on a single work out unit embedded in their organization ("captive") and doing most of the work related to their NPLs credit recovery. Outsourcing is often treated as a secondary measure to use in case there are peaks of work: banks exploit it only in order to temporarily handle the need of some extra capacity. Several reasons may then explain the tendency of keeping the work out unit "captive" inside the bank rather than fully outsourcing it. Firstly, NPLs are still accounted for in the total amount of asset owned by the bank (even if they are of poor quality), so that managers may not be eager to transfer them because doing so would reduce the bank's size, at least under a total assets perspective (this is particularly true for the Head of the work out unit, whose influence and relative level of power is usually linearly related with the overall amount of the gross value of NPLs).

More importantly, as long as NPLs are still sitting in the bank's balance sheet and influence its Profit and Loss statement, it may be possible to keep them at their current book value and avoid, or at least postpone, the losses connected with the almost inevitable write offs related to their true sale.

The tendency of doing nothing so that to avoid any short term negative impact on the Profit and Loss statement of a bank should definitely be avoided and, as it will be explained later in this chapter, even when assets are managed by an internal unit, they should be recorded at their "true" and "realistic" fair value. Sometimes, it is argued that the internal management of NPLs may be justified in the case some of them have some kind of "strategic" or "relational" value: keeping the assets inside grants control over them—so it goes the argument, and therefore the bank may want to handle them internally to be able to get all the associated benefits. Lastly, banks possibly still rely on internal set ups because they do not have an effective framework that could help them in choosing the optimal solution. This chapter aims at explaining how such a framework could be built and such a choice could effectively be made on the basis of few pragmatic performance indicators.

4.2 The Internal "Embedded" Set Up

A bank carrying out at least part of its workout process internally has to decide how to structure its workout unit, which could be either fully embedded within its organization or treated as a separate legal entity (with or without a full banking licence). In the first case, the workout unit will be part of the bank in a narrow sense. This may lead to some issues in terms of level of independence, since under this set up it is more likely that different parties in the bank will try to influence the unit so that it would work in a way that is in line with their own goals. This is why the unit's position in the overall corporate structure should be carefully identified. From an organizational perspective, the unit could report to the Chief Lending Officer (CLO), to the Chief Operating Officer (COO) or to the Chief Risk Officer (CRO)—in some extraordinary case, it could also report directly to the CEO. The choice is not trivial, because the different Operating Officers have very different objectives, which they will also try to pursue through the workout unit that they end up being responsible for, affecting the way the recovery process is then carried out. In other words, it is an easy bet that the focus of the unit will be aligned to the overarching targets of the relevant Chief.

Specifically, as said, if the workout unit reports to the Chief Operating Officer, it may have an incentive to optimize its cost income. This can be achieved with greater recourse to variable costs, for example thanks to the assistance of third party sub servicers and collection agents. As already mentioned, a greater level of outsourcing is desirable in many cases, but external workout is not necessarily the best solution in all kind of situations. A bank could, for example, choose to handle internally the NPLs that it knows and can manage better, in order to maximize the recovery rate on them. In other words, while cost optimization is undeniably a good thing, efficiency should not come at the cost of sacrificing too large a portion of the recoverable amount of a loan, as there is an obvious trade off between operating costs and the NPLs' cost of risk. Indeed, if the external servicers do not perform well enough, the cost of credit arising from sub optimal recovery rates may become so high that it greatly outweighs the benefits from lower operating costs. On the other hand, if the workout unit reports to the Chief Lending Officer, it could push for the maximization of recoveries, regardless of the impact on the cost structure. This may lead to a situation where an excess of fixed costs determines a very rigid operating costs structure and high operating leverage.

There is hence a trade-off between the cost of credit and the operating costs, and the organizational structure of the workout unit may tilt the focus in one direction or in the other according to the organizational set up but also given the specific phase of the economic cycle. This is confirmed by the fact that in good phases of the cycle, the incentive may be to give the responsibility of the workout unit to the COO in order to contain costs, even if this results in a lower level of recovery; whilst, in negative phases of the cycle, the tendency could be to put the increasing volume of the overall NPLs under the responsibility of the CLO. Finally, the workout unit could also report to the Chief Risk Officer. This solution is less common and it is usually adopted in cases where the overall bank is subject to heavy restructuring. Under these circumstances, there may be even cases where the CEO is directly in charge, in order to direct the workout activity in a way that is consistent with the rest of the bank's "change or die" turnaround process.

4.3 The Internal "Separate Legal Entity" Set Up

In a second approach to the internal management of NPLs, the bank could decide to set up a workout unit that is legally separated from the bank (even if, in most instances is fully owned and controlled by the bank). In this case, the issue of interferences and potential manipulations from other divisions of the bank should be more limited, since the workout company would have its own board of directors and separated governance structure. An independent board could focus on a more comprehensive approach to credit workout, striking a better balance between the targets of efficiency and recovery rate. Also, the top managers of the work out could be better incentivized.

An independent workout company can be set up in a number of possible ways, with or without a banking license and with or without the direct ownership of the assets being collected. The unit can hence be designed as a mere service center, or operate independently as a principal counterpart (and therefore profit center—even if, more rarely, it could be a profit center also in the case of its being a mere service center). In the first case, its performance can be measured and controlled by the banking group on the basis of Service Level Agreements (SLA), which can specify target rates and metrics to achieve, as part of the incentive scheme of the management (and for the calculation of the success fees paid to the independent legal entity). A workout company that operates as a pure profit center is rather a rare case in practical terms, and it is unclear what the hurdle rate to calculate the success fees for the loans it manages should be. In the second case (with the work out unit owning the assets), the way a "principal" workout company is usually set up is by having the parent bank contributing the NPLs, and associated liabilities, into a new vehicle initially fully owned by the same bank—e.g. creating a sort of bad bank inside the group. This process is relatively fast as it requires no third party negotiation and the creation of minority/majority stakes, and it allows the bank's shareholders to fully participate to the NPLs future, potential recovery.

4.4 Captive "Deceptive"

Regardless of the fact it is carried out through a fully embedded unit or through a separated company—owning or less the NPLs—a captive workout unit, and its related processes, tend to be opaque. In fact, managing NPLs internally gives rise to two main issues, as already mentioned in the paragraphs above. The first issue relates to the fact that the unit may not work on the basis of market prices and hurdle rates. This is connected with the fact that banks may choose, when managing them internally, to keep NPLs at book values which are consistent neither with market prices nor with reasonable fair values. It follows that it is not clear what the target recovery rate should be for the legally separated, but still fully bank-owned, workout company. The second issue is that captive units are subject to the interference of other parties of the bank. At a first level, this fact can affect the focus of the unit (the before mentioned trade-off between efficiency and recovery). More worrisome though, is the possibility that key decision makers may urge the unit to adopt policies aimed at preserving the NPLs accounting value, even when doing so hinders the chances of maximizing their economic value (as rightly expressed by the "net present value" of the expected recoveries, net of associated expenses). The aim of preserving the accounting value of the NPL books could thus incentivise behaviours aimed at delaying or avoiding the accounting recognition of losses and foster the reporting of inaccurate or unrealistic values for the NPLs managed. In this sense, a captive workout unit is a deceptive one, or at least potentially so.

4.5 The External "Outsourcing" Set Up

A cleaner and more "market driven" solution may therefore involve the full externalization of the work out activities, or at least the heavy use of independent, professional players acting in the open market. There are several options for outsourcing part or most of the credit work out activities. If the bank wants to have a

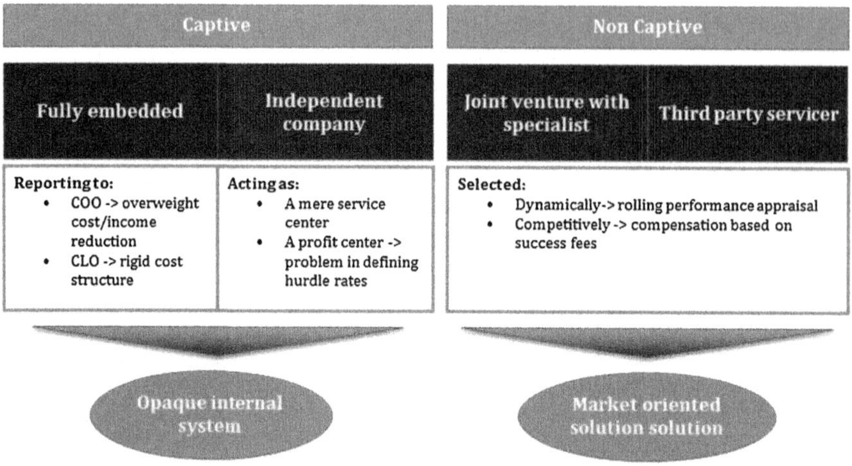

Fig. 4.1 Captive versus non-captive: an un-obvious decision. Credit management set ups. *Source* Own illustration

higher level of involvement in the recovery process, and retain some direct involvement in the governance—if not in the management—of the NPLs, then the credit workout unit could be developed via a Joint Venture with an independent specialized player—usually leaving to the third party the majority stake of the company. Alternatively, NPLs could be allocated dynamically and competitively to few selected third parties. These could be selected on the basis of a rolling performance appraisal and their compensation could depend heavily on success fees, paid on the basis of the extra recovery achieved given the hurdle rates set by the initial contractual agreement. In both cases, the bank should be able to maximize the upside coming from better than expected performance (see Fig. 4.1).

4.6 Model Selection: Three Factors to Consider

Given that several options are available for the set up of a workout unit (be it captive or non captive) it is critical to understand the pros and cons of such a variety of set ups. The different models can actually be explained as a function of strategic choices on a few key elements.

Firstly, the optimal set up will vary depending on whether the bank wishes to retain its NPLs ownership or not. For example, if it decides to outsource the recovery process, the bank usually remains the full owner of the NPLs; but it could also consider selling first the NPLs portfolio, leaving the decision on whether and to whom outsource their servicing to the end buyer. On the other hand, by creating a separate legal entity and ceding its NPLs to it, a bank loses the direct ownership of the assets, but it could retain the full ownership of the new company—or it may decide to retain just a minority interest—for deconsolidation purposes, or nothing at all.

The second issue to consider is then related to who should have the organizational responsibility for the credit work out management. A very basic approach would be to have a general manager handling the recovery process. In the case of a credit workout unit, as already explained, the responsibility could be assigned to an Officer within a function (CLO, COO, CRO or CFO) or to an independent Officer reporting directly to the CEO in order to limit the potential interferences from the various divisions. For any of these options there are obviously pros and cons, with potential interests not fully aligned with the final object of shareholders value creation. As mentioned, a COO (Chief Operating Officer) lead credit work out unit could become too focused on operational efficiency and cost income targets, not maximizing the potential value that is recoverable from the loans. On the other side, a CLO (Chief Lending Officer) lead work out unit could have the incentive to postpone the recognition of the troubled situations and related losses, as they would entail the implicit recognition of the past mistakes made by the CLO in the underwriting process. A CRO (Chief Risk Officer) lead credit work out unit could, instead, become too focused on the regulatory and compliance aspects of these activities and pursue the optimization of the regulatory capital absorbed by the NPL portfolios, at the cost of the sub optimization of the recovery rates (expressed in net present value) that could be attained through the credit collection. Similarly, a CFO lead credit work out would likely become too focused on the capital management and financial aspects of its activities—keener to do true sales or financially structured transactions, with a much lighter focus on the industrial aspects of the activities. Finally, as for the option of the credit work out unit reporting directly to the CEO, it is basically a non solution—e.g. a residual choice actionable when all the others have failed, or just in quite extraordinary circumstances, with the risk that this direct reporting will become a “non reporting” (as the CEO will be busy on a number of other issues).

For any of these options, it should however be remembered that if a separate legal entity has been created for carrying these activities, either bank owned or third party owned, it would follow that it will have a separate board of directors legally responsible for the credit management activities. This further level of governance and responsibility usually implies further costs and more internal “bureaucracy”, but also an extra layer and guarantee of strict monitoring, control and effective decision making on the most critical parts of this peculiar business.

Once a decision on the ownership of the NPL assets and on the organizational responsibility has been taken, a final, third step should consider clarifying the role of the workout unit in terms of the expected contribution to the Profit and Loss of the bank. In fact, the assessment of the performance of the credit work out unit and the target it will have to pursue will change dramatically depending on its economic role aimed for. Leaving aside the still numerous cases in which the unit has no specific position inside the bank, so that its activities cannot be clearly recorded and evaluated, the main distinction is between units that act as mere cost centers and units that are potentially profit centers. In the first case, the workout process is simply seen as an inevitable price to be paid in order to reduce the cost of credit. If this is the case, the focus of the credit work out unit will likely be the optimization of the costs for the unit of NPLs worked out, in order to limit as much as possible the drain of resources connected with the recovery (this option is therefore often associated with a direct report to the COO). On the other hand, a credit work out unit as a profit center will likely focus on a more comprehensive set of aspects, and its performance will be mainly assessed based on its ability to reach recovery levels which are higher than the set hurdle rates—no matter what the costs associated are (this option may be associated with a reporting line to the CLO).

Figure 4.2 shows the possible models that can be obtained by combining different approaches to credit management organizational responsibility and

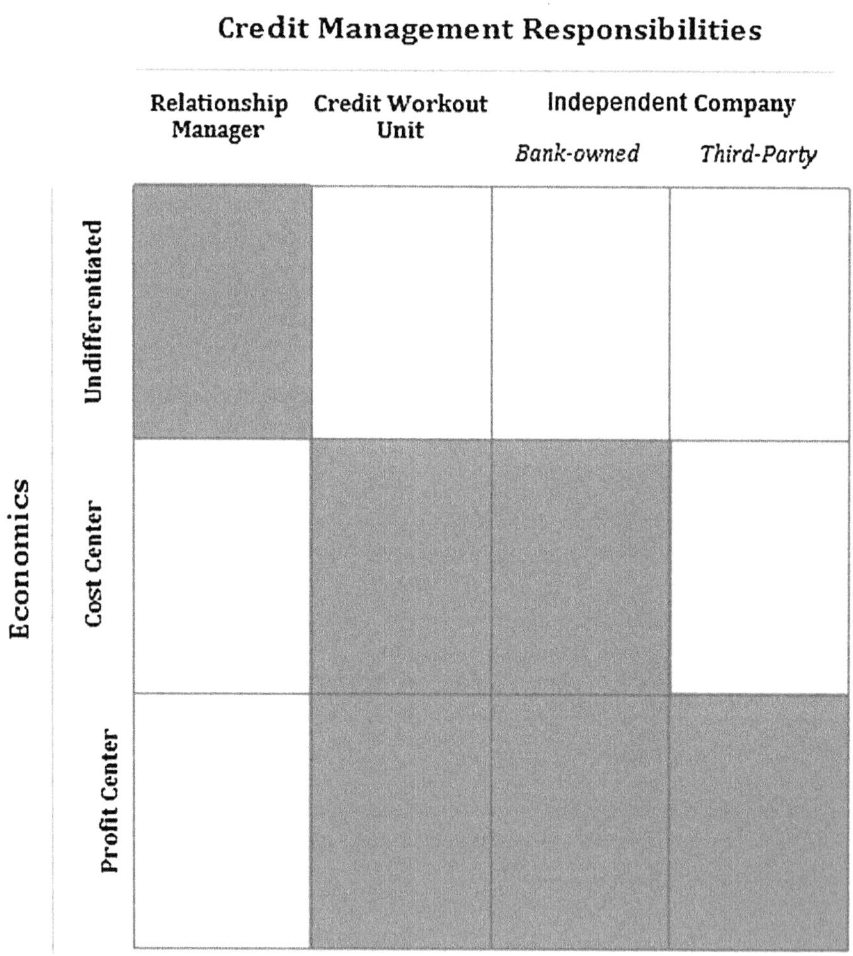

Fig. 4.2 Credit work our responsibilities and targets. *Source* Own illustration based on internal analysis

business/service center unit roles and targets. The shaded cells are those for which the resulting combination makes sense from an economic perspective. At a first level, the workout process could be assigned to a relationship manager and carried out as an undifferentiated activity. This solution is excessively naïve and the rising relevance of non-performing loans, both in terms of volumes and of complexity, has made handling the recovery process impossible for a manager who is not highly skilled and experienced in this kind of business. At the other extreme, a third-party owned independent company must necessarily act as a profit center in order to survive and prosper in the open market. The residual cases to consider are the ones of an internal credit unit and of a bank-owned independent company open to the possibility of choosing whether the workout process should be treated simply as a drain of resources (cost center) or as a revenue generating activity of its own (profit center).

4.7 Bank Owned, Independent Credit Work Out Units

Given the variety of set ups already mentioned, it is clear that some of these are more interesting than others under a credit work out management perspective, because they are more open to the possibility of developing a holistic and active workout strategy (our suggested "WHAM" approach). Looking at the independent third party owned credit work out option, it is clear that whilst a bank can structure methods to choose the optimal level of outsourcing and identify the best external servicers, the responsibility for the actual recovery process in this case is ultimately in the hands of the external provider. On the other hand, if a bank decides to keep the workout process captive, it must choose the best set up to do so and put in place procedures that should guarantee an effective recovery process—in other words, ensuring that these processes develop as holistic and active as possible, notwithstanding the original "captivity" of this credit work out. For this option, the optimal set up could therefore be the ones limiting the constraints coming from the fact that the unit is captive, and hence possibly deceptive (opaque, not fully transparent, not well incentivized) are minimized—considering the best trade off between conflicting goals (the optimization of the cost income—pursued by the COO; and of the recovery rate on the NPLs—pursued by the CLO).

With regards to the multiple options previously discussed, having an "independent" workout company (even if fully owned by the bank) that acts as a fully independent profit center is probably the best solution to achieve both objectives: on one hand, the fact of having a separate company with its own board of directors should reduce interferences and increase transparency and the correct set of incentives; on the other hand, if the company aims at being profit center it will try harder to balance different goals, optimizing both the cost income and the recovery level.

From an organizational and governance perspective, an independent credit workout company could then be created within the group or as a third company participated by the bank—and jointly owned with other third parties (industrial, technological or financial partners).

In the first case, the bank contributes its NPLs and associated funding liabilities into a new vehicle within the group which is still fully and directly owned by the bank. The resulting "bad bank" can then structure different portfolios of loans in line with the composition of the related collateral and considering all other kinds of segmentational criteria as already discussed. This "bad bank" will then be able to structure NPL portfolios with different risk/reward profiles that it could sell to different investors according to their risk/reward preferences. While this solution is relatively easy and fast to implement because it requires no formal alliance or Joint Venture with third parties, it exposes nonetheless the bank to possible accounting losses on day one, because the assets will need to be re-valued at their fair price once contributed to the new legal entity, and then at market values once the selling process gest to the final transaction stage.

An alternative solution is then to consider the spin off or demerger of the full book of the NPLs of the bank. In this second case, the "bad bank" containing all of the NPLs of the bank is proportionally de-merged in favor of the bank's shareholders: two shares are issued and exchanged to the bank's old one and with quite different risk/reward profiles. This process is more complex, also from a legal and regulatory point of view, but it allows shareholders to keep participating to the full NPLs recovery, whilst on the other side offering them an easy way to refocus their financial resources just on the good bank (they can sell the bad bank's shares and reinvest the proceeds in the good one). Moreover, the non performing assets may be sold not as single dossiers or portfolios, but through the simple exchange of the shares representing the ownership of the bad bank—allowing therefore more liquidity and transparency from day one—ideally through a regulated stockmarket.

The alliance or Joint Venture options could then be pursued in different ways, according to the two quite different structures presented. In the first case (new company created and initially fully owned by the bank), the alliance or JV will be directly negotiated by the bank as parent company of the credit work out unit—it could potentially reach a full deconsolidation only if, at the end of the process, will sell to a non related counterpart the majority of the shares of the new credit work out (or "bad bank") company, which, in this case, has been built as the servicer and as the owner of the bad loans. In the second case, the alliance or JV could directly happen via the stock market (assuming the bank's shares were already floating in the stock market and that also the two new shares—substituting the old one—will be let floating freely on the stock market as representative of the ownership of the "good" and "bad bank" being created with the spin off or demerger of the original bank. It will therefore not be directly controlled by the management of the (remaining) good bank, who will keep acting as a totally different company (even if, on day one, this company will happen to have the same shareholders of the "bad bank" one).

Whatever the financial and governance structured solution adopted, ensuring the effective implementation and management of the workout unit managing the bad loans is fundamental. This can be done, as already explained, by defining and

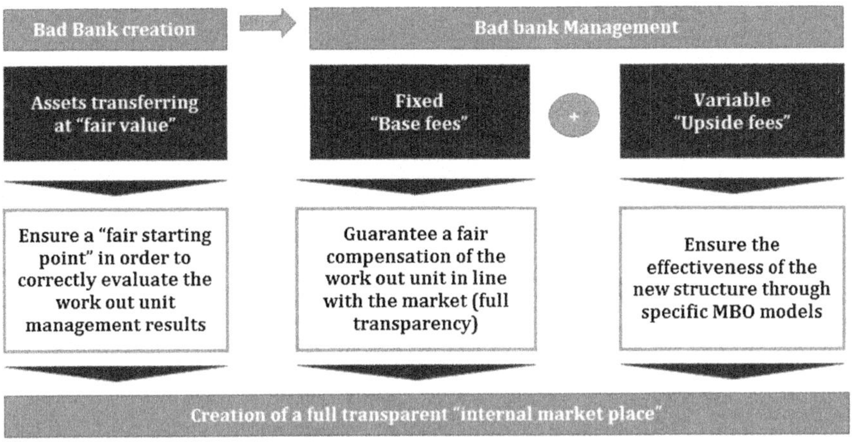

Fig. 4.3 An internal marketplace for the bad bank. *Source* Own illustration based on internal analysis

putting in place a transparent process which should significantly reduce, if not eliminate, the distortions that may characterize a captive NPLs credit work out unit. Developing a transparent "internal market place" is therefore essential (see Fig. 4.3): the idea of the "internal marketplace" is basically the idea of creating a system that is strongly linked to actual market prices and hurdles, so that to provide the right incentives to the management of the workout unit—no matter who its shareholders (whether the old ones of the parent bank or the new ones buying a stake in the stockmarket) are and will be. In order to build an internal marketplace governing mechanism, at the very first stage, when creating the workout company, the NPL assets being transferred should be revalued at fair value and short terms hurdles should also be set at market values, even if the haircut applied will probably cause a loss for the bank, should a market transaction happen at all. And this is important for two reasons. Firstly, as already said, a bank should not postpone inevitable write-offs (as sometimes is the case derived from the use of excessively optimistic "fair values"), but it should give a clear representation of the true value of its NPLs (probably in between the over-the-cycle fair values and their short term market values).

Secondly, reporting and contributing assets at their fair value will ensure that the workout company begins its operations from a fair starting point. But also, considering continuously what the market prices are will provides an incentive to the managers of the work out unit so as to optimize its recovery rate, because their work will be assessed comparing continuously the expected net present value of their recovery activities versus the market price which could be immediately obtained through a competitive true sale to a third party. If, on the other hand, assets were contributed at a book value way higher than the fair and market prices, the credit workout unit would almost certainly record a loss, due to the impossibility of recovering such "optimistic" values: its managers would therefore end up being less motivated to perform all kind of holistic and active processes, therefore sub optimizing the actual recovery obtained. Ultimately, the independent credit work out company, set up as a "profit center", would end up reporting losses or near zero profits—challenging its own legitimacy and going concern existence in the medium-long term.

Once the contributing values of the NPLs portfolios have been set, another critical element to consider in order to create an internal marketplace system that works, is how to structure a proper and effective compensation system for the credit workout company. In the case of an external provider this would be usually based on a combination of a fixed fee and a variable, performance related one (usually a share of the over recovery performed, given the set hurdle rate and calculation methods that should be based on the assessment of the net present value of the recoveries). The same structure should be applied when the process is carried out internally, if the bank really wants to create an "independent" credit work out unit (even if fully owned by the bank itself), in the belief that this is ultimately the best solution to ensure the maximization of the recovery value for its shareholders. In both cases, the fixed fee component should cover most of the direct costs and some part of the variable ones of the credit work out unit—and they should be negotiated in line with the market benchmarks even in the case of the independent work out (or bad bank) fully owned by the bank: this would in fact allow to compare the cost of the internal processes with the one offered by external suppliers, so as to make sure that the internal workout is neither too expensive compared to external alternatives, nor underfunded. Additional compensation in order to create an incentive system could then be based on an upside fee related to the extra recovery on the assets managed or sold, for example by calculating the difference between the net present value of the recovery strategy and the NPLs current market values. We may call the extra recovery (mutating an idea from the asset management industry) that a credit work out unit can generate in an uncorrelated way vis a vis the market and in a sustainable way as the "alpha" of this kind of business—and the "alpha" should basically drive the payment of the success fees. A more extensive discussion of this "alpha" factor and on the ways to basically build selectively competitive platforms to deliver it high and consistently through time is then developed in the next chapter of this book.

Chapter 5
Developing a Credit Work Out "Alpha Platform"

Abstract Credit work out could be interpreted, at a stretch, as a very special component of the asset management industry. As such, both "beta trackers" and "alpha players" could be viable business model—the first aiming at big volumes, economies of scale and low cost bases; and the second one aiming at creating over performance (better recovery rates) which are sustainable over time and uncorrelated versus the performance of the market. In order to build an "alpha platform", few distinctive capabilities are identified and analyzed, starting from the governance and organization, the processes and procedures, the data management and development of unique algorithms and, finally, strong talent teams. A number of trade-offs needs to be managed among these distinctive levers and a monitoring report (dashboard) could be usefull in analyzing the performance of both the internal and external partners being used in the different parts of the value chain.

Keywords Beta tracker · Alpha player · Alpha platform · CLO · COO · Industrialization · Monitoring · Strategy definition

5.1 Beta Trackers and Alpha Players: A Snapshot of the Asset Management World

In the previous chapter, we have carefully analyzed all the possible set ups that banks can implement in order to efficiently manage their NPLs portfolios and all the main elements that can influence such a decision. Whatever the governance and organizational options undertaken, the credit work out unit has to take accurate management decisions on its managed non performing assets in order to maximize the potential recovery and minimize the losses. Therefore, credit work out becomes de facto—latu sensu—some sort of asset management company, whose performance and value created strictly depend on the strategy adopted and on its operational set up as a platform offering services and performing activities associated with the credit collection. On this basis, some kind of reference to the asset

C. Scardovi, *Holistic Active Management of Non-Performing Loans*,
DOI 10.1007/978-3-319-25363-3_5

management industry could be useful to explain the approach that the credit work out unit has to have in dealing with the challenge of ensuring the optimal recovery on its managed NPLs. In this paragraph different asset management models will be therefore quickly described and compared, and their application to the credit work out business will be explained.

In fact, when it comes to traditional asset management business, two are the categories usually referred in the market: the so called "beta trackers" and the "alpha players". The "beta trackers" are those entities that, after having identified a meaningful reference benchmark, will try to pursue a payoff very much near the one of the benchmark—basically replicating the composition of the market portfolio and taking actions that are very similar, if not utterly equal to those taken by the market at large. A classical exemple of the concept of "beta play" is given by the ETF (Exchange Traded Funds), which follows the performance of a market index, or of other kind of discretionary indexes by basically building "pro quota" a portfolio which is the very same "replica" of the ones for which the indexes are built and monitored. Being relatively less risky than other kind of active strategies (in fact, beta tracking is also named "passive strategy"), the "beta tracker" players focus mostly on reaching economies of scale in order to maximize their efficiency and therefore their relative performance, reducing management costs as much as possible through standardization).

On the other side there are the "alpha players", characterized by an active management of their investment portfolios. Their goal is not just to minimize their management cost (usually a less critical target for them), but eventually to create over performance on their investment in an un-correlated way with the market and then making this sustainable across the economic cycle. Their building a superior platform, able to produce "alpha", is usually pursued by attracting and retaining the best talents, or building specific, data driven proprietary algorithms, or investing in cutting hedge technology that allows some spikes in the strategic asset allocation or in the tactical stock picking, but also developing cutting hedge policies and procedures for their investment activity. Alpha players could then be broken down into two different subcategories: pure alpha players, who are benchmark aware but implement some kind of strategy that allows them to differ quite significantly from their reference index over time, and the "systematic alpha" ones, that represent some kind of middle ground between a purely passive and a pure active alpha strategy.

Beta and alpha strategies can then greatly differ for what concerns their risk return profile. While for beta trackers a lower relative risk is counterbalanced by a generally low expectd return, or anyway no overperformance compared to the one realized by the benchmark, alpha strategies should allow to beat the reference index. At the same time, they present a greater risk of downside in the investment. Even if more uncertain, alpha strategies could however allow the investors to gain more from their invested funds because expertise and managerial skills are employed at best to take investment decisions and asset managers are usually compensated with a success fee (or some kind of "carried interest" on the over-performance realized with the managerial activities). The same reasoning should apply to credit work out units that could either be "beta trackers", just focusing on the efficiency of the cost income and basically "following the market", in terms of approach, activities, people, technology etc. Or be "alpha players" in the way they are trying to consistently beat the market, providing over recovery through times on its managed NPL portfolios, on the basis of a few (or combination of) quite specific competitive advantages.

5.2 Different Ways of Becoming an Alpha Player

Broadly speaking, "alpha players" in the credit work out business could be classified according to one or more of the four following competitive dimensions they could be pursuing (see Fig. 5.1).

5.2.1 Talent Driven Alpha Playing

The first competitive dimension of alpha playing is the so called "talent-driven" one and it is based on the superior abilities and skills of the management of the work out, who is supposedly able to create a durable overperformance through its active management of the non performing assets. In a competitive model which is solely based on this dimension, most or all of the overperformance would be totally dependent on key people and therefore linked to their staying with the company

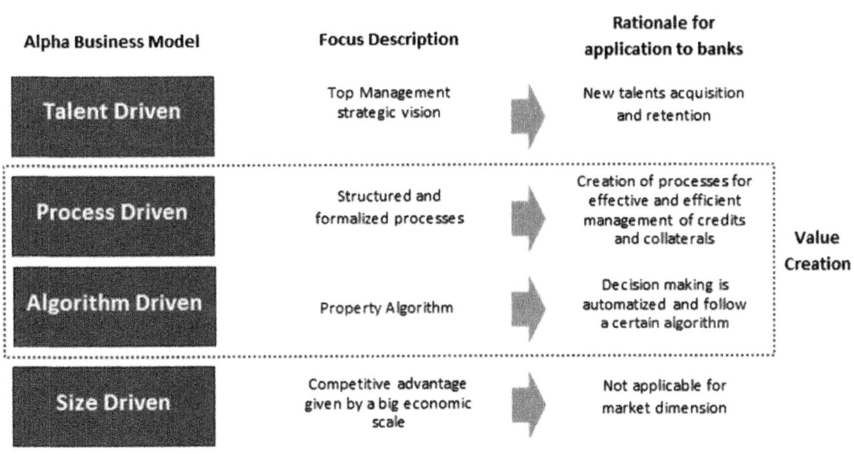

Fig. 5.1 Alpha strategies for credit work out

overtime. In this situation the ability to not only retain the best "old" managers, but also to acquire over time "new" ones and of incentivising them at best becomes critical: new talent acquisition allows to create over time multiple reference points within the organization. The high focus allocated on managing people and their skills can just help in managing a situation in which there is the constant risk that these talents might leave the firm, possibly hurting its whole performance and competitive advantage. Therefore, it is often the case that the talent acquisition and build up of "soft" skills thought the organization does not always create sustainable long term goodwill for the company, as the risk of its dissipation through time remains high. A credit work out unit that wants to uniquely pursue such an alpha playing driver should therefore manage this lever very carefully to understand how to better lock the overperformance brought by its key talents.

5.2.2 Process Driven Alpha Playing

A second dimension that could allow credit work out units to pursue alpha playing strategies is linked to their internal "way to do it". It is based on the concept of embedding into the organization the "optimal recovery" and "performance maximization" mindsets, by defining structured and formalized processes and procedures, which can be followed at any time in order to pursue the best recovery and credit collection. This model would clearly limit the overall inter relationship between over performance of the credit work out and the retention of key talents—as it was discusses in the previous example. More specifically, when applied to a credit work out unit, the process driven alpha playing dimension requires to design and build a set of robust processes and procedures for the effective and efficient management of both credits and underlying collaterals. An example of such a model would be a credit work out unit that entrusts teams of specialist with the mandate to manage the most complex and potentially recoverable value rich portfolios of loans, while leaving to "standard" supporting functions or to third parties the most basic activities—to reduce costs per unit and reach economies of scale. From this rationalization and alignment of resources (best resources allocated to the most promising value recovery opportunities), the work out could increase the internal experience curve and minimize the costs incurred at the same time.

5.2.3 Algorithms Driven Alpha Playing

When the best recovery strategy and approach is defined by formulas, the alpha playing dimension being pursued is sometimes referred as algorithms based. A specific proprietary algorithm is usually created from the analysis of multitudes of data carried out by the credit work out unit, so that it uniquely defines management decisions and the best credit collection and recovery strategies. This alpha playing approach depends therefore critically on the identification of an effective and efficient algorithm that should create and sustain through time the over performance of the credit work out. Being numerical and formulaic in nature, this approach will give a much lower weight to management skills and decisions and it is therefore much less reliant on the talents of the company (whilst it still rely heavily on processes, as the output produced by the algorithms are then translated into action through the semi-automated processes of the credit work out). In fact, a credit work out that applies the algorithm driven dimension to deal with its non performing assets usually tries to improve and automate decisions as much as possible by following certain and objective mathematical rules. This approach allows then to the credit work out unit to put in place a better filtering system on the potentialities of its NPL portfolios and to decide more carefully, for any one of them, whether to outsource or not. Differently from the first, talent-driven dimension, both the process and the algorithms driven one allow a greater and less volatile build-up of goodwill.

5.2.4 *Scale Driven Alpha Playing*

The last business model that can be implemented to pursue alpha playing strategies is driven by size and by the full industrialization of the operating capabilities of the credit work out unit. In this case, the competitive advantage is created mainly by exploiting a scale that competitors are not able to reach or manage and therefore by positioning the credit work out unit at a "cost to income" level that cannot be easily matched in the market. The same objective of positioning the company on an operational efficiency curve that is unmatched in the market can also be pursued through the industrialization of its operating model—as commented in a later chapter of this book. With the scale driven alpha playing strategy, costs are minimized over a quite large amount of assets managed, and learning and experience curves are exploited, and the over performance to the end customers of the credit work out unit (the owner of the managed portfolios of NPL) is then ensured by passing through some of the cost efficiencies that are just not attainable by the rest of the market.

This model is not pursued very often, as markets for credit work out services are usually very fragmented and given the tendency of banks to retain internally most of these activities. Therefore, the two models that represent the best solutions for credit work out units are the process driven and the algorithms driven ones. This is because they allow the work out to operate in an effective and efficient way, allowing, most importantly, the build up of stable goodwill through time.

5.3 The "Trade off": Cost Optimization Versus Recovery Maximization

When banks have to manage their own troubled credit in a captive credit work out unit, two main situations, as already mentioned, could materialze. If the work out unit reports to the Chief Operating Officer (COO), it may have the greatest incentive to optimize its "cost to income", with greater preference given to variable costs (as generated by the use of third party sub servicers and collection agents). This approach has often in practice lead to the sub optimization of recovery rates and of the value recovered for the banks' shareholders, as in most of the phases of the economic cycle the cost of credit ends up weighting much more than the operating costs. On the other hand, when the internal work out unit reports directly to the Chief Lending Officer (CLO), it will push for the maximization of recovery rates, no matter how rigid and heavy the cost structure could become (see Fig. 5.2). In practice, even when the work out unit reports to the CLO, banks tend to focus mainly on the reduction of operating costs—which is the effect most immediately visible and certain (versus the benefit provided by an extra recovery that could happen much later in time).

It follows that in such situations banks tend to give up on strategies of recovery that would require instead greater investments and operational costs to actively improve the chances and magnitude of the recovery on defaulted assets. In other words, the main priority and focus of the internal credit work out unit too often revolves around the efficiency of the collection process more than on the effectiveness of the recovery itself. But is this apparently insourmountable trade off really written in stone? Or maybe at least partially avoidable through the careful and

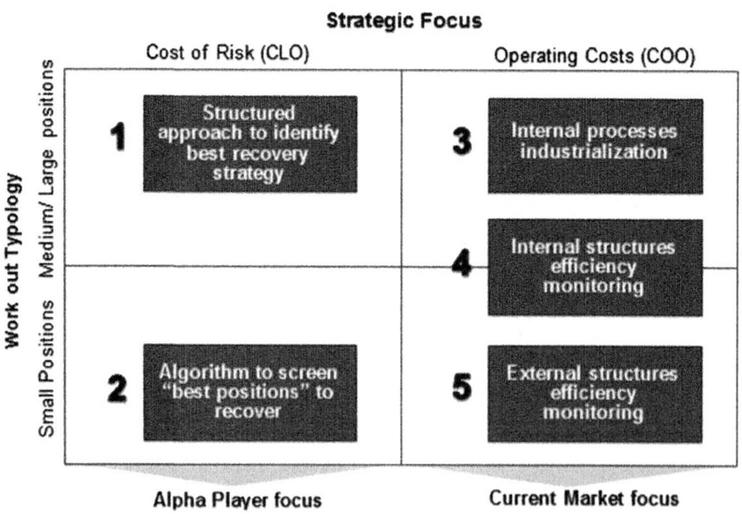

Fig. 5.2 Five actions to overcome a trade off

creative design of work out platforms built to perform as alpha players? In our experience, we have seen opportunities for credit work out units to become alpha players by focusing on both recovery maximization and cost optimization—overcoming some of the old taboos that lead to the above mentioned "trade off".

If we take into consideration the Italian market (for independent credit work out units), the current focus appears to be mainly on the containment of operating costs despite an increase in the cost of credit: do the bare minimum and as cheaply as possible—maybe because is the way to optimize the results for the next quarter—even if at huge costs for the future. The result is that whilst the current market trend in NPLs accumulation is strictly upward, the total recovery achieved on those loans has only slightly increase. This is a worrisome sign, because it shows that a management approach on NPLs that aims at their sole cost optimization may end up in widening over time the gap between the NPLs managed and the actual performance on them. On the other side, an alpha playing strategy would decrease the cost of risk whilst choosing the best recovery strategy and workout scope, therefore limiting the costs of the platform and enhancing at the same time its operating performance. An appropriate strategy for overcoming this trade off, and pursue at the same time cost optimization and recovery maximization would then rely on five actions:

1. Identifying the best recovery strategy;
2. Screening the best position to recover;
3. Industrializing the front-to-back processes;
4. Monitoring the internal structures;
5. Monitoring the external structures.

These five actions are presented and discussed in the following paragraphs.

5.4 Defining the Best Recovery Strategy

As mentioned, the first action that has to be taken is to find the best strategy in order to deal with the defaulted loans in the best possible way. This topic goes back to the definition of the segmentational criteria that then create different clusters of NPLs that can be used to map out all the different and possible permutations along the credit recovery value chain. These permutations can be used as a reference to identify the best strategy to deal with them. As already commented before, choosing an appropriate management strategy for each category of NPLs is crucial in order to not only limit the waste of resources, but also to maximize the chances of getting back as much as possible from a situation usually very difficult. We now provide two examples on how to handle complex and different positions and find the best strategy to deal with them—overcoming the traditional trade off between "cost to income" minimization and "recovery rate" maximization.

5.4.1 An Equipment Leasing Work Out Case Study

In the first example, we refer to the world of leasing equipment work out (see Fig. 5.3). In leasing, differently from a banking loan, the bank is already the owner of the good being financed (in this case, an equipment used by the end customer). Therefore when the debtor defaults, the bank has the right and opportunity to repossess the asset that was at the centre of the leasing—with no need of a specific judicial procedure. In the case of equipment leasing, the underlying asset could vary a lot, given the etherogeneity of the goods usually financed. Equipment goods that are leased could in fact be very specialized, or even built ad hoc for the end customer, and therefore difficult to deal with and usually very illiquid (there is almost no secondary market for an equipment built ad hoc for a given customer). If the credit work out unit uses an undifferentiated approach in managing them, could end up with significant operating costs and potentially very low recovery rates. On the other side, if it defines a "smart" recovery strategy may end up minimizing its operating costs and increasing the expected recovery rate—therefore overcoming the above mentioned "trade off".

In our case study, we have classified the equipment goods that have to be handled by this hypothetical credit work out unit according to a matrix that maps them by their level of marketability and their potential upside (here defined as a multiple of the potential investment further required to put them on sale). A certain remarketing strategy (for reselling the good and recover as much cash as possible) is then defined for each sub category of goods identified.

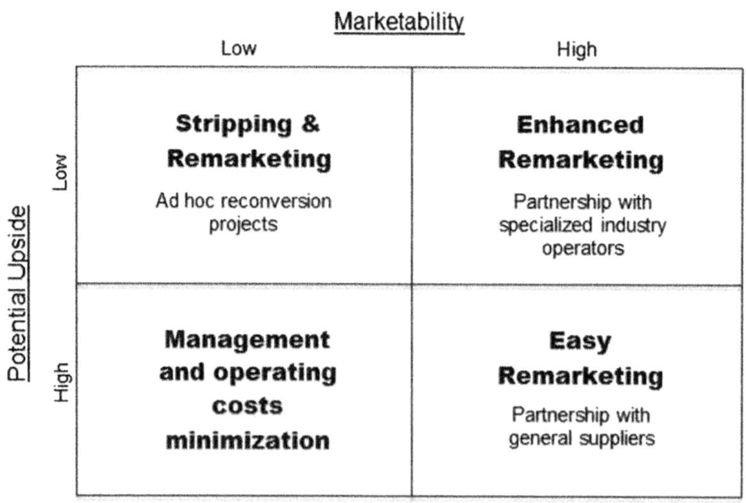

Fig. 5.3 Equipment leasing remarketing strategy. Remarketing approach segmentation matrix. *Source* Internal analysis

In our example, we firstly identified a category of equipment goods that have a current low marketability but a big potential upside: these assets are those that could, for example, be placed within complex production sites. For them, an appropriate recovery strategy could be defined as "stripping and remarketing": the bank could invest in "ad hoc" reconversion projects with the aim of recovering the marketability of these goods, to then resell them at a later stage and with a significant value added. Usually these goods are just a small percentage of the total leased assets, both in terms of number of files and relative value. In a second category, we find instead equipment goods have both low marketability and low potential upside: for them there is not much a credit work out can do, and the best strategy could just be the one that manages them only with the goal of minimizing the operating costs (given that the expected recovery is near zero anyway). Usually, these goods comprise around half of leased equipments dossier, but they are also very limited in value. Also in this case, the optimization of the "cost to income" is pursued without negative impacts on the recovery rate, therefore overcoming the traditional trade off.

In a third category, equipment goods can have a low potential value compared with the investment required to manage them, but be very liquid nonetheless. In this case the credit work out should opt for an "easy remarketing" strategy, that requires low use of extra resources, but that is still able to provide acceptable returns. This kind of remarketing can be done in partnership with general suppliers. Examples of this category of goods are gym equipments or basic machineries. Also in this case there is no apparent trade off between the targets of cost to income and recovery rate.

Finally, in a fourth category, we find the best situation for the credit work out, when both current marketability and potential upside are quite high (see Fig. 5.4). These goods are usually limited in number in the balance sheet of the bank, but have a high average individual value: an example could be the earth moving

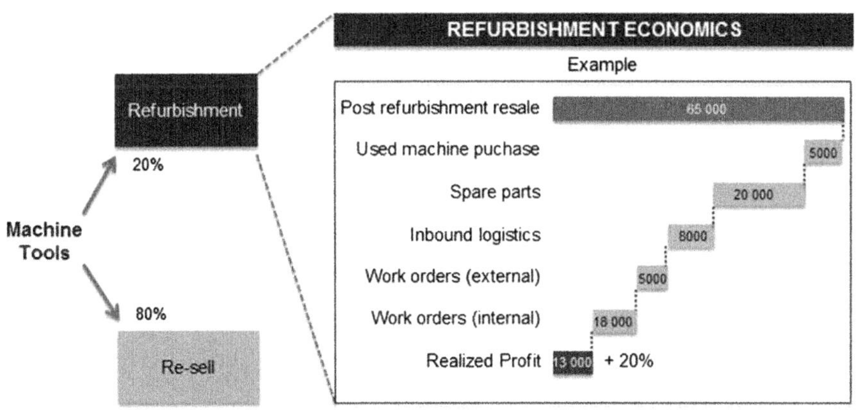

Fig. 5.4 Refurbishment, remarketing and resale. Leasing equipment example. *Source* AlixPartners experience

machinery. It is clear that the credit work out must prioritize the management of these assets, since they represent a profitable opportunity, and most of the extra costs should be readily justified by the extra revenues that could be reached by the re-sale (therefore optimizing the recovery rate without harming the cost to income). An ideal strategy could then focusing on an "enhanced remarketing" effort, often done in partnership with specialized industrial operators.

Figure 5.4 shows a real life example in dealing with a leased equipment machinery tool and how an "enhanced remarketing" strategy could create value for the bank.

In a more traditional approach, the credit work out unit could just try to re-sell this kind of asset straight away: acceptable returns would then be easily achieved due to the strong and resilient value of the asset, while the high marketability would allow for a fast sale that does not require particularly high transaction costs. Despite appearing profitable, this plain vanilla strategy does not however allow to exploit the full potential of the recovery process. In fact, a remarketing strategy that requires the refurbishment of the asset and then its subsequent resale could result, as shown in the example above, the optimal one. As seen in the example in Fig. 5.4, on a post refurbishment resale, the credit work out could achieved a resale price post refurbishment that is much higher than the price that it would get in the plain vanilla approach.

5.4.2 Real Estate Backed NPL Case Study

A second example can be related to some real estate assets that were used as collateral for loans that have now defaulted (see Fig. 5.5). The bank in this case could prioritize some proactive action in the management of those assets in order to preserve, maximize and speed up their recovery value. Three kinds of managerial

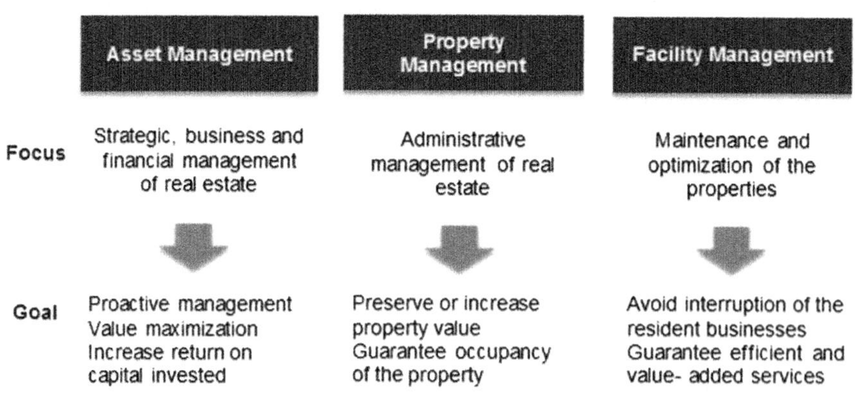

Fig. 5.5 Active management of a real estate collateral. Real estate example. *Source* Internal analysis

actions are, at first sight, possible and we can group them under the labelling of "asset management", "property management" and "facility management".

With the asset management actions, the bank usually focuses on the strategic, business and financial management of real estate assets. The bank aims therefore at achieving three goals at the same time:

- Maximizing the real estate asset value;
- Increasing the long term return on the invested capital;
- Managing the fundamentals of the property proactively.

Real estate asset management is, among the three kinds of actions, the one potentially most effective, as it allows to treat the real estate asset as an investment and to look for the maximization of its current and prospective yield. In order to manage a real estate collateral in this way the organizational unit of the credit work out needs to carry out an analysis of the profitability of the asset, redefining its industrial and business plan, with the idea of identifying the "to be" status of the asset that creates more value versus its initial "as is" one—even considering such things as changes in destination, in the design and in the refurbishment or technical set up of the building, and the way it is finally commercialized and brought to market to meet the potential end buyers.

With the property management actions, the focus is instead centered on the administrative management of real estate. The objective is now shifted on the preservation of the property value (if possible, also on its marginal increase through time), given the state of the property itself and the level and quality of its occupancy. This type of action aims at managing the property in a profitable way, without a specific financial target in mind (neither value maximization nor exit opportunity are sought via the activities of property management). An effective property management of a real estate asset is then realized through the following steps:

- Defining the budget for buying/selling properties;
- Promoting the active search for tenants/buyers;
- Analyzing the lease maturities;
- Planning and starting up commercial campaigns;
- Preparing administrative and accounting reports, on collection of rents; on technical, legal and administrative documents; and on payment of taxes.

For what concerns the last kind of action, regarding the facility management of the real estate assets, the focus is really on the maintenance and cost optimization of the property. Therefore, no breakthrough added value is created via this kind of action, but returns are achieved ensuring a proper continuity of the activity already operated on those assets. The objectives of such facility management activities are the maintenance of the properties so as to avoid any interruption of the renting businesses, and to guarantee an efficient service to the end users of these properties.

5.5 Defining the Best Position to Recover

The second action that has to be taken to overcome the trade off concerns the creation of a screening process on the positions that have to be recovered internally. The aim of such a procedure is to better select those portions of NPLs portfolios that each bank (or the independent credit work out unit) manages internally versus the ones that will be outsourced.

Generally, as already explained in the previous chapters, a bank prefers to keep managing internally the positions with the highest recovery potential, whilst outsourcing the remaining: this allows to maximize the returns on the recovery and optimize the cost structure—in turn, what is left is allocated to third parties which are nonetheless eager to take on the remaining. Therefore a sort of "food chain" is developed in the market (see Fig. 5.6). The first player (in our case, the bank that originates the loans) chooses what NPLs to externalize and keeps the "best" ones for its internal workout. In turn the second player, that is now allowed to process the

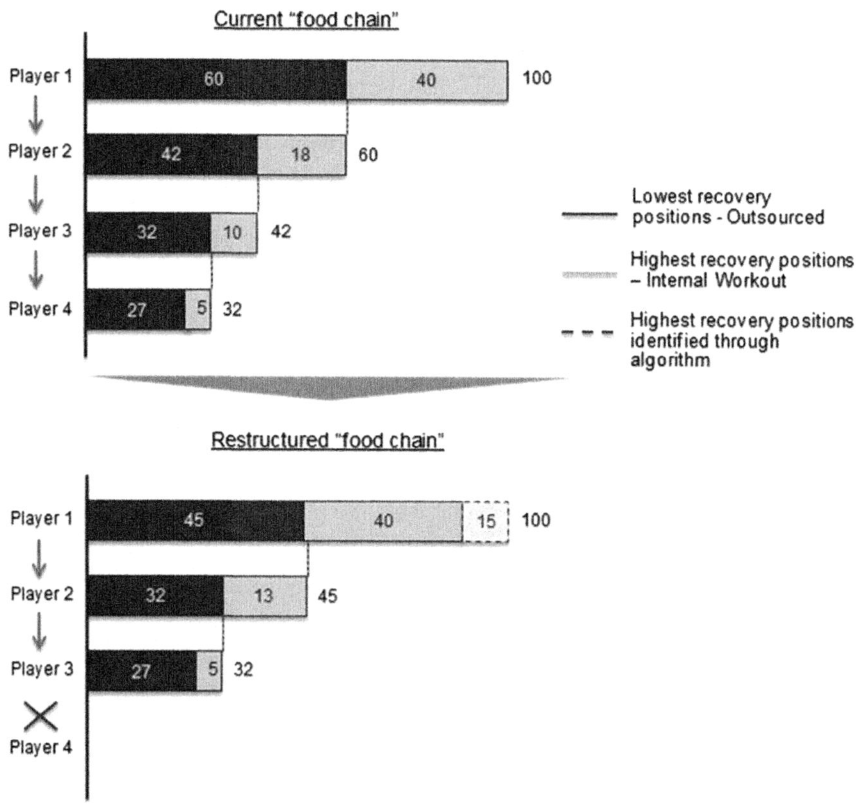

Fig. 5.6 The credit work out "food chain". Current and restructured "food chain". *Source* Internal analysis

leftovers of the first player, decides what part of its positions to keep and what part to pass over to a third player, and so on. Basically, each player tries to maximize the return by selecting the best NPLs to be worked out among the remaining relevant positions and according to some standard criteria (more recent vintage, bigger size and more secured positions are preferred over older, smaller and unsecured ones). This leads in turn to a "waterfall process" of selection: the number of loans passed on to the following phase is lower and lower, until only the very marginal positions with an almost irrelevant recovery prospect remain.

What we can infer from this process is that currently a lot of "food" goes wastes. If the originating bank were able to properly identify all the positions (or at least a bigger amount) that have a high recovery potential, it could keep them for its internal workout management and therefore achieve a higher return. A way to implement a proper and effective method for screening positions and to look for the better recoverable ones is through a proprietary algorithm—as already described. Therefore an alpha player credit work out should maximize the profit by developing algorithms, using non-standard criteria (beyond the "common sense" selection variables) and leveraging the best applied analytics techniques to "mine" and understand all the big data available. This approach could then help the bank in selecting a number of high recovery positions that can be kept for internal workout—extending this process across the small ones as well. In this way not only the workout of troubled portfolio would be optimized, but also the "food chain" would be shortened and made it more efficient for the benefit of the overall economy. Figure 5.6 exemplifies how the "food chain" currently works and how algorithms would transform the process for the better.

5.6 Industrializing the Internal Capabilities

The next three further actions are aimed at the optimization of the cost structure (and are typically under the control of the COO). The industrialization of the operating model and of its related capabilities implies the rationalization of all the workout processes so that the bank is able to handle a bigger quantity of loans without a correspondingly linear increase in the resources used up (see Fig. 5.7). In particular, the bank will be able to achieve an increase in its productivity followed by a speed up in its recovery time by putting into practice a number of actions aimed at simplification, specialization and standardization. In a traditional approach, most of the processes and of the workout functions are assigned indifferently to the people and organizational units working in collection. Therefore no function is truly focused on few selected activities and most of the collection teams and units tend to operate in competition, and not really in a complementary way. Ultimately, a lot of resources risk to be wasted in the work carried out by functions with no specific added value and with no clear competitive advantage. A redesign of the operating capabilities of the credit work out aimed at fostering the specialization of the activities and their standardization would, on the other side, allow to

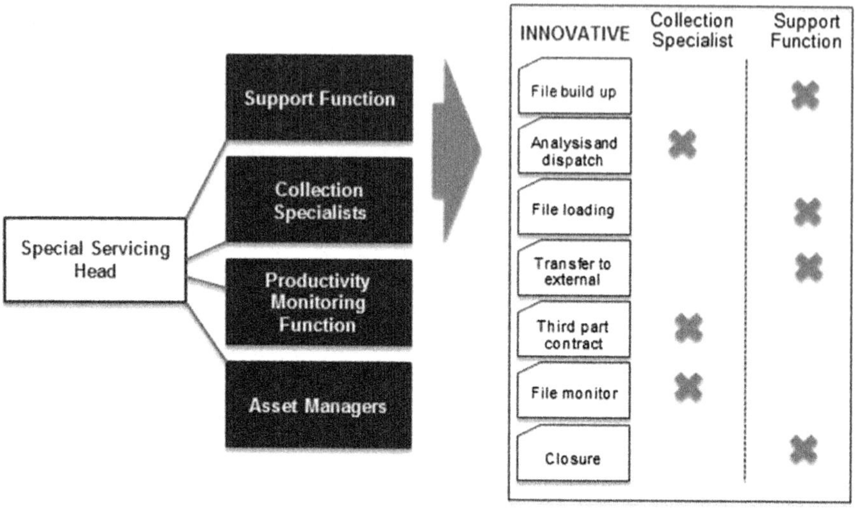

Fig. 5.7 Breaking out the credit work out "value chain". Processes industrialization, example. *Source* Internal analysis

break down workout functions between collection specialists and a support function teams. The latter would provide services in a standardized way, following a pre-defined template and file loading, covering all the basic functions that are nonetheless needed by the collection specialists.

The collection specialists would then work on the remaining activities that could have greater added value and that require more focalization. Collection specialists would then be divided according to their expertise, type of activities or categories of NPLs managed. The assignment of a certain type of activity to different specialists would therefore augment the experience curve of the employees, allowing for further cost optimization and better performance in the overall recovery achieved.

Figure 5.7 summarizes how an internal credit work out could be broken up in different organizational units, with few examples of further industrialization.

5.7 Ensuring the Effective Monitoring of Internal Structures

Streamlining the internal processes and related resources of a credit work out unit is certainly the most effective and direct action that can be taken in order to optimize its operating costs in the short run. However, all kind of short term, easy "quick wins" should also be considered in terms of their related risk of back firing in the medium term—with costs required to perform the activities bouncing back through inefficiencies, errors and reworks or—as typical—lower recovery rates.

In any case, a credit work out unit should be able to continuously assess whether the systems it has in place are efficient, in order to make appropriate corrections if it identifies some dysfunctions that are already visibile or could just back fire in the mid term. This continuous assessment can be achieved by constantly monitoring both internal and the external structures which could complement or substitute the former, with different methods and depending on the final aim.

For what concerns the internal efficiency, a credit work out unit could evaluate this on the basis of few key dimensions (see Fig. 5.8). For each of them, the work out unit should build a specific set of key performance indicators (KPIs), which are strongly related to the evolution of the connected variable and can help in monitoring this last one. Such indicators should be constantly updated in order to promptly identify whether the system in place is actually effective. KPIs should

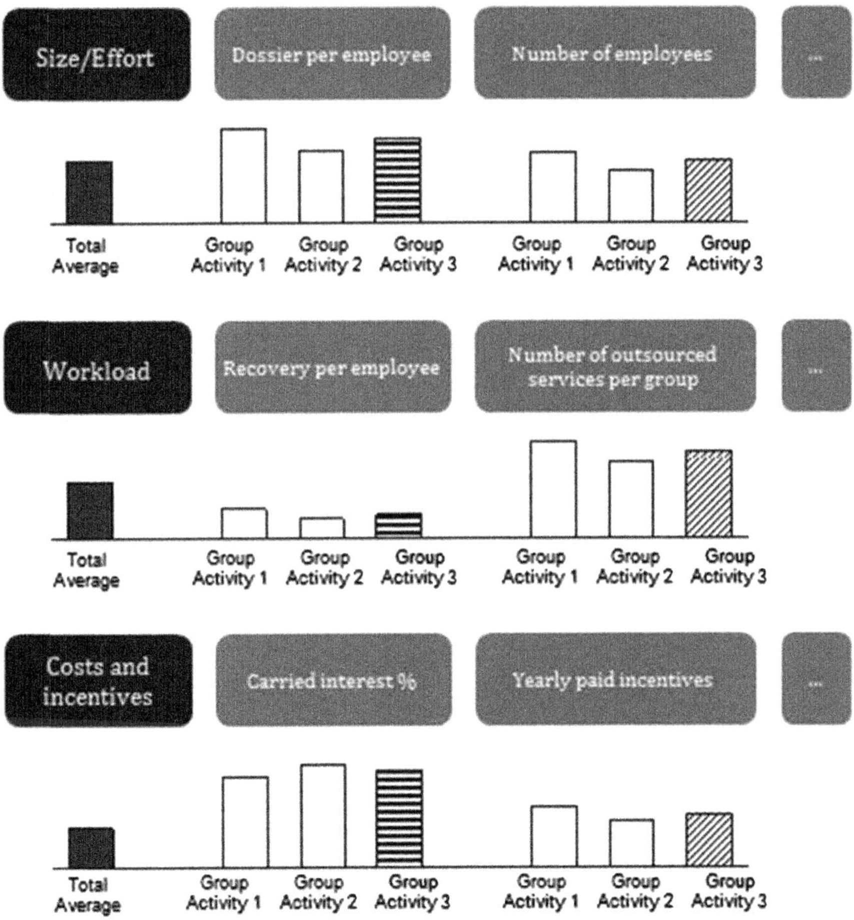

Fig. 5.8 Monitoring the productivity of a credit work out. Internal workout structures productivity monitoring. *Source* Client example

then be compared across internal working groups in order to identify if the performance is aligned among them and in what way they contribute to the overall level of the work out unit. If the performance is disappointing, the credit work out unit should consider conducting potential improvement actions. Figure 5.8 exemplifies how the monitoring process is then set up.

For example, a first relevant dimension, the size of the effort, could be evaluated on the basis of its associated KPIs (number of employees, dossier per employee, etc.). By considering parameters such as the recovery per employee and the volume of outsourced services per group activity, a credit work out unit could assess whether it has the right level of resources to manage the expected workload. If for some groups some of the indicators in these areas are far above or below the average, for example if the number of dossiers per employee is too low or too high, the credit work out unit could then consider rightsizing the affected group by staffing less or more people on it. It could also decide whether it should review its business model, for example by increasing or reducing outsourcing on specific groups. The cost structure and the incentive systems can also be revised, depending on the results coming from the analysis of the associated KPIs. The list of relevant dimensions provided is anyway not exhaustive, and many additional factors could be considered. In any case, a proper and more detailed valuation should be carried out under a well defined framework, following a structured approach, such as the one suggested in this section.

5.8 Ensuring the Effective Monitoring of External Structures

The efficiency of external structures should also be assessed and continuously compared with the performance realized by the internal ones. A bank should therefore put in place an objective system to evaluate the performance of its own credit work out units versus the ones of different, external servicers, in order to be able to choose the best partners for its workout activities. An effective and holistic way to do so is developing a "balanced scorecard" that would assigns a numeric score to each external structure on the basis of several elements (see Fig. 5.9). Obviously, the most relevant of these dimensions is how well the provider performs in financial terms (e.g. as net present value of the recoveries achieved). In this regard, the key element to consider is the total value recovered, net of related expenses and considering the time value of money; with respect to this factor, performance could then be evaluated by looking at the total performance gap, in terms of difference between the value recovered by the servicer and a target value, which could be either a fair value, a liquidation value or something else depending on the options available at that point in time to the bank, and considering the IRR (internal rate of return) associated with the recovery.

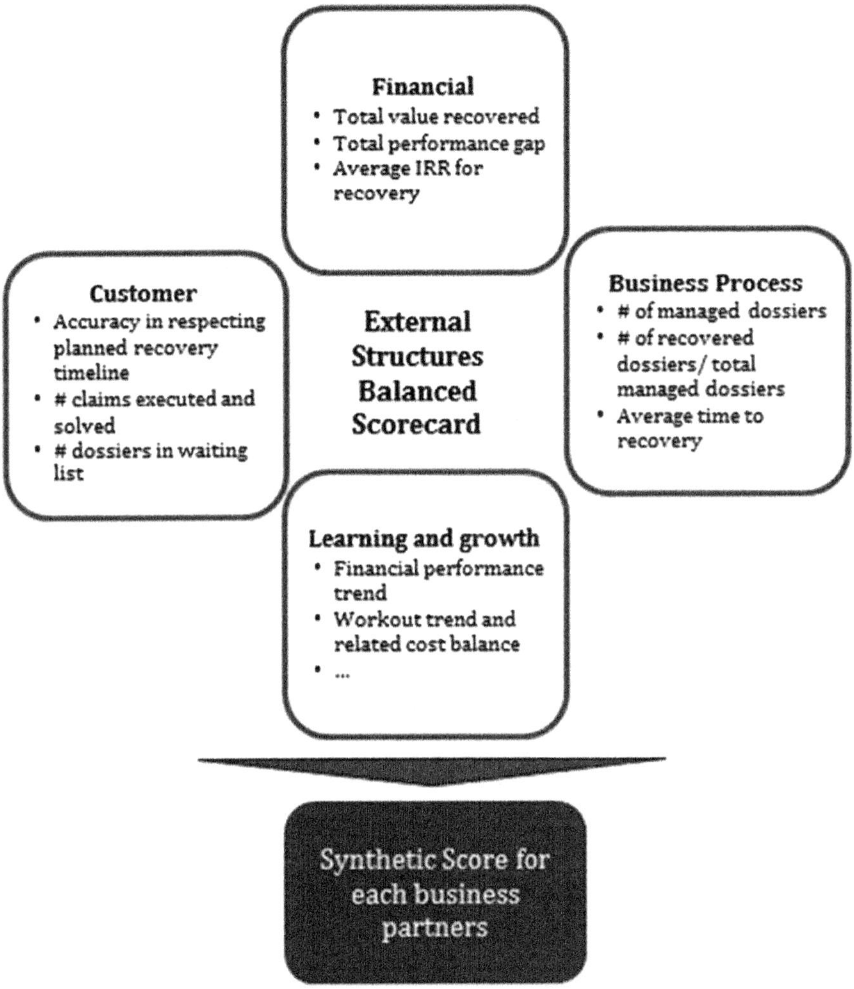

Fig. 5.9 A balanced scorecard for the credit work out. Example of balanced scorecard. *Source* Client experience

While the financial performance is undoubtedly important, judging on this factor alone may not be enough to provide a clear picture: a more comprehensive set of dimensions has therefore to be considered. For example, a bank may want to look at the business processes of an external provider in order to assess its efficiency, reliability and transparency. This implies carrying out an analysis similar to that conducted for monitoring internal structures; processes should be evaluated by looking both at the success rate (in terms of proportion of managed dossiers that is actually recovered, net of related costs) and at the timing (in terms of average time taken) of the recovery.

A third element that could become relevant is the kind of customer relation the servicer has got with its clients—the banks and other financial investors owning the NPLs. This aspect is more difficult to evaluate in numeric, objective terms, but looking at some parameters such as the number of claims executed, or dossiers in a waiting list and the timeliness versus the planned timeline, may help understanding whether the external provider, besides being efficient, is also reliable.

Finally, it is worth to remember how valuations should not be carried out under a static perspective. This means that credit work out should constantly update their scores in order to make sure their performance does not deteriorate through time without being immediately reflected into their reporting systems. By doing so, it may be possible to identify some trends both in terms of financial performance and of improvement in cost efficiency, possibly deriving from volume effects and economies of scale that need careful assessment and immediate action. A bank may then consider including a separate value to account for the benefits coming from a credit work out unit's improvement in learning and growth. Once a synthetic score is obtained, business partners can also be ranked in order of efficiency, and loans can be outsourced to the best providers in a dynamic and competitive way. A periodic review of the performance of external structures should then allow to progressively consolidate their volumes on the best partners. This should improve workout effectiveness and potentially lead to a cost reduction given some discount connected to the volume effects and to the greater negotiation power obtained. Moreover, the continuous assessment should increase the competition among partners, which will do their best to remain at the top of the rank.

Chapter 6
Developing an Holistic and Active Credit Work Out Unit

Abstract Developing a WHAM (work out: holistic and active management) effective approach is the key target of any captive or non captive credit work out—and ideally an effective way to become an alpha player: using more heterogeneous and comprehensive management tools (holistic) and focusing on a time to speed approach that anticipates most of the foreseeable issues (active). A WHAM approach can start with the design and creation of the credit work out unit itself, but also envision in parallel "crash program" initiatives and external accelerators for the medium term. Few of these—from the real estate agency, to the real estate owned company, are discussed in this chapter with specific reference to the steps to be considered for their build up and to the pros and cons to be considered by the credit work out and by the parent/client bank at large.

Keywords Work out: holistic and active management · WHAM · Crash program · External accelerators · Real estate agency · REOCO

6.1 Developing a WHAM Approach

In the previous chapters, we have analyzed and explained the importance of an active workout approach in the management of increasingly bigger amounts of non performing loans. We went through all the actions the banks should take in order to deal with NPL portfolios according to the different phases of the credit lifecycle (see Fig. 6.1). We now want to better assess how to set up such a holistic and active approach to credit recovery in the best, most efficient and effective way. There are in fact three potential main areas of work to design, develop and built to completion, (whilst at the same time managing the urgent situations) a "WHAM" (work out holistic active management) unit as market best practice. As a start, the process involves the actual set up of the unit—this could take up to approximately six months and would include the organization of the NPLs database, the development of a new organizational and operating model. At the same time, crash

C. Scardovi, *Holistic Active Management of Non-Performing Loans*,
DOI 10.1007/978-3-319-25363-3_6

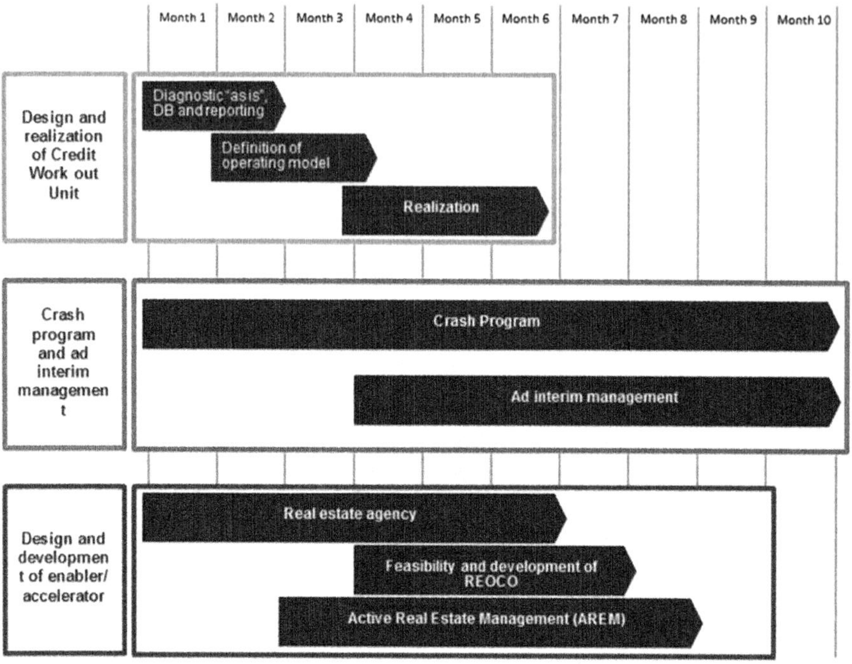

Fig. 6.1 An action plan for the build up of the credit work out. Timeline of the set-up of a Credit Workout Unit. *Source* Own illustration based on internal analysis

programs and the definition of ad interim roles must be consider in order to manage all the urgent and extraordinary operations needed from the beginning onwards. Simultaneously, an optimal setup of a credit workout unit could include the development of the so called "accelerators", needed to speed up and facilitate the processes that may lead to credit recovery maximization. As shown in Fig. 6.1, the accelerators could include initiatives such as the "real estate agency", the REOCO (real estate owned company) and the active management of underlying real estate assets.

In the following paragraphs, we will analyze more specifically the steps that have to be considered in order to build up a well organized, efficient and effective credit workout unit.

6.2 Design and Creation of a Credit Workout Unit

As anticipated in Fig. 6.1, the set up phase aimed at the creation of a credit workout unit of excellence could be divided in three main steps. In a first step, a diagnostic on the "as is" situation is usually completed in few weeks, followed by the definition of the target "to be" model. These phases can be shortly summed up as the initial assessment of the bad assets to be worked out and of the organization and quantity/quality of the available resources. They should also lead to the definition of the structure and organizational model to be implemented, and finally to the proper start up of the credit work out unit. The diagnostic on the "as is" situation should also allow to build a database containing all the relevant information on the troubled loans to be managed. It is in fact critical to define and organize the "raw material" (that is the NPL portfolios and their underlying collaterals) and to identify the "final product" that will result as outcome (in terms of expected recovery rate and generated value), and organize the available resource in the most efficient way.

The main steps that have to be followed for the design and realization of the database are:

- Analysis of all the available information, followed by the definition of the structure of database of NPLs and linked collateral (both real estate and other categories of assets);
- Analysis of indicators for each single credit that has to produced, analyzed and managed;
- Analysis of "second options" for real estate assets in order to verify the consistency among the appraisal, the fair value and the market value—the information stored by the database;
- Analysis for each macro category of collaterals, of their value decay curves through time;
- Analysis of the KPIs concerning other intangibles and the operational/reputational risks that could be driven by the NPL managed: quantitative and qualitative information should be included and some judgmental analysis for the most critical situations.

Afterwards, a productivity dashboard could be developed and continuously updated, leveraging the analysis already performed in the previous step. This productivity dashboard would allow:

- The monitoring of the underlying productivity and of the support instruments introduced;
- The definition of specific KPIs on productivity (examples are cash flow/resource, number of files/average time/resource, NPV per Euro of ICT costs/HR costs, etc.);
- The definition of the "generated value" for each dossier or cluster of dossiers (net present value and IRR versus a minimum hurdle rate have to be taken in consideration);
- The implementation of KPIs and "key risk factors" that can be connected to each dossier: macroeconomic, industrial and sector specific elements have to be defined;
- The definition of the best liquidation strategies and of their related timetable;
- The introduction of sensitivity analysis and control checks to evaluate the potential impact of the changes in each scenario and in any key risk factor (as

changes in euribor, inflation or real estate cycle) also aimed at potentially envisioning hedging/insurance strategies.

After having built a useful database and having organized the indicators to assess the potential outcome that could be extracted from it, the next step would require the segmentation of the credit portfolio and the definition of the perimeter and of the overall scope and mandate of the credit work out unit. The actions to be taken would therefore be the following:

- Definition of the target portfolio and ultimate scope and mandate of the unit;
- Identification of the key variables for the valuation of the underlying assets: these will be differentiated for the main kind of asset related relevant database;
- Analysis of the NPL portfolios and of the collateral assets with specific focus on size and loan to value (credit quality, status of the asset, expected recovery rate).

Following an organizational diagnostic, a more detailed human resources analysis should be carried out, and followed by the analysis of the potential third parties partnerships. These steps should include the following activities:

- Mapping of the current processes for credit work out management: main activities, phases, teams and people, organizational units and structures;
- Organizational assessment: this step concerns the analysis of the different organizational units involved, and the analysis of the mismatch at the level of a resources/activities matrix;
- More detailed human resources diagnostic for the management of troubled loans: roles, skills and profiles have to be examined and matched with those needed;
- Assessment of any emerging gap in human resources compared to the desired target and assessment of the potential partnerships with third parties for the management of the phases of the processes or of the kind of collaterals which are not within the scope of the workout unit (e.g. in case it has been decided that all the small ticket files have to be outsourced);
- Definition of a specific perimeter for the activities that will be outsourced;
- Benchmarking and selection of external operators.

The second step requires to further defining and building up the model that will stand as the target structure of the credit workout unit. Therefore, the organizational structure, the internal processes, the procedural rules and the human resources needed must be specified and organized. The definition of the target operating model of the credit work out will then require both the analysis of the external service providers (outsourcers) and of the capabilities that should be built internally:

- On one side, an analysis of the key aspects of the main market operators on credit collection available in the market will allow to better focus and compare the potentially available organizational structures, their processes and related incentive systems;

- On the other side, the internal definition will need to dig further in terms of operational aspects concerning the day to day activities of the credit work out unit:
  - Its set up as either legal entity or organizational unit inside the banking group;
  - Its reporting to either the CLO, the COO or others;
  - The ownership of the non performing assets (versus being a pure servicer);
  - The mandate of the management with regards to the main expected targets;
  - Its economics (e.g. its set up as either a pure service/cost or profit center).
- In case the bank is considering the idea of developing the credit work out platform to address the open market and develop a business per se (e.g. serving some of the clients of the bank or other smaller banks), the definition of the potential market and of the related go to market plan could also be beneficial for the future development plan of the unit;
- After having looked at the external environment where the workout unit will operate, the internal structure must be taken into consideration, giving particular care to its internal functioning processes, its interrelations with the rest of the bank and the pricing rules, with:
  - The definition of the main internal processes and related interconnections;
  - The definition of the pricing rules on the internal transfer of the assets (at either the fair value or the market value—or in between) for the valuation of the recovery targets and the set up of the hurdle rates that will define the incentive schemes;
  - On this basis, the definition of the base remuneration (retainer) for the management of the NPL portfolios and of the success fees that should be benchmarked with what is paid by the market to third party independent credit work out platforms;
  - The definition of the incentives model that maximizes the commitment of the management and is based on results (e.g. based on the overperformance realized);
  - The formalization of the mechanisms for the functioning of the credit workout unit.

The definition of a specific human resources model is also an important aspect that allows the matching of the skills and experiences of the people available with the actual needs of the credit work out unit. For such kind of task, the analysis usually performed entails:

- The definition of the target profiles (past and expected role, general abilities, technical skills, direct experience, etc.) and their sizing and related costs, given the target model;
- The definition of the resulting gaps and the following recruiting plan aimed at fulfilling the key positions (alternatively, the planning for an internal

reallocation of people across roles and tasks, as an alternative or as a complement to the external recruiting activities);
- The definition of the training gap that will need to be overcome to make sure the credit work out has all the skills required for the optimal management of its recovery activity.

Finally, in the design and set up phase of the credit work out, a key activity should be focused on the clusterization and industrialization of the recovery strategies. This phase refers to the already mentioned process of dividing NPL portfolios into homogeneous clusters, based on their main characteristics and on whether they are leasing or banking positions. This would involve:

- The analysis of the credit portfolio and of the main categories that could be used for creating homogeneous clusters, and the definition of all other kind of other useful segmentational criteria: by ticket size, counterparty, type of collateral, residual value, geographic allocation, vintage, judicial versus non judicial process undertaken etc.);
- The analysis of the peculiarity of the business for each cluster and the first identification of the possible ways to generate value (then defining the best recovery strategy), differentiated according to the underlying asset, the counterparty, the phase of the credit lifecycle of etc.;
- The design of a matrix concerning the strategies for the management of each cluster previously identified, referring specifically to the best re-marketing strategies for each kind of collateral: for the real estate, for example, the remarketing optimal strategies could involve the creation of "accelerators" such as the real estate agency and the REOCO.

Once the previous steps of work have all been cleared, the project of creating a new credit workout unit can move to the execution phase. We usually break down this into two kind of activities, some of them routine or "standard" and some of them "extraordinary" in their occurrence and "urgency". The standard activities involve all the actions that have to be taken in the daily management of the unit. They involve also a trial phase that is aimed at testing the real effectiveness of the unit via:

- The selection of a number of medium—small ticket files (not managed through an ad hoc program) that can be used to test the normal functioning of the credit workout unit;
- The training of the people and teams on the financial and industrial management of NPLs and of their underlying collaterals—with specific reference to real estate skills;
- The monitoring of the results of the pilot through the a specially designed dashboard;
- The fine-tuning of the model in its key components: internal processes, recovery strategies to be implemented, reporting and incentive systems to be set up and considered etc.

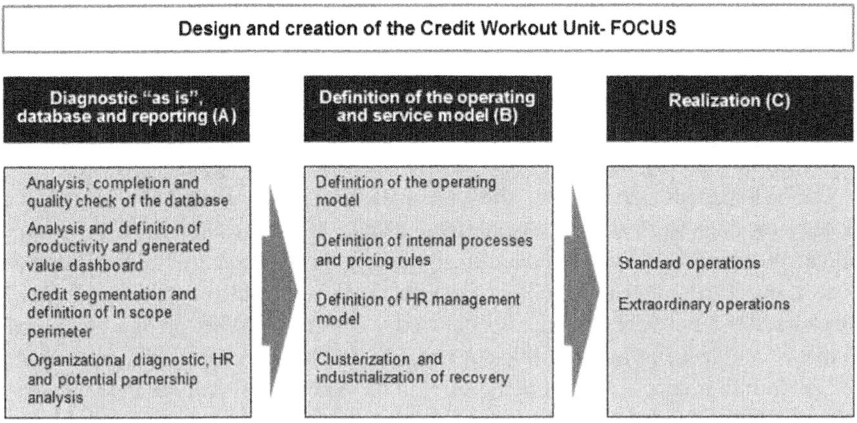

Fig. 6.2 Main phases for the set up of a credit work out unit. Steps for the setup of a Credit Workout Unit. *Source* Internal analysis

In parallel, some extraordinary or one-off activities may be needed and could require a quick implementation. Some typical example of such activities could be:

- The identification of some possible segmentation criteria for the portfolio aimed at the definition of "ad hoc" transactions that are being discussed with selected counterparts;
- The development of feasibility analysis for the sale of some portfolios, with specific determination of the different tranches of types of loans and related collaterals;
- The selection of the main buying counterparts (private equities, hedge funds, or others) and the execution of speedy sale process, usually involving a limited number of counterparts.

For the sake of clarity, Fig. 6.2 summarizes all the main steps already discussed that have to be taken into consideration in order to build and create a credit workout unit of excellence.

6.3 Crash Program on the Most Urgent Situations

Quite often, whilst designing and planning for the creation of the credit workout unit, it is useful to consider a "crash program" to be executed in parallel, to address the most urgent situations and critical files. The "crash program"—usually developed with the support of external, turn around consultants—can aim and be limited to the active management of a few files, or extend its reach to the overall NPLs portfolio, playing de facto as a sort of "ad interim management" structure, until the new credit work out unit is properly set up and fully up to speed, with a new management appointed and fully in charge of the day-to-day activities. The crash program is usually focused on the analysis and management of the positions with highly critical issues and/or important residual value. Therefore, on step one, the dossiers that will be the target of the crash program will have to be identified and prioritized. And for any dossier, an estimate of the expected value of the recovery and of the resourcing needed to realize this will need to be quickly clarified.

The selected positions must then be analyzed in detail and an operational strategy for their work out must be defined: as part of the feasibility analysis, some indications should be given to determine the best recovery strategy for each targeted loan, in order to optimize the NPV of the portfolio being actively managed. Given the characteristics of each NPL, a specialized team should be set up and organized, so that it can deal in the most efficient and effective way. As part of that, for each non performing loan, an action plan needs to be designed so that the best recovery strategy, both judicial and extrajudicial, can be implemented. The ad interim management, which sometimes becomes part of the scope of the crash programme carried out by an external consultant, should be focused on specific organizational role, whilst the new credit workout unit is still being designed and implemented. The areas that potentially could require an ad interim role should be identified by comparing the most relevant activities and the available internal resources (with detailed indication of their key skills and experiences). In particular, if a gap between required and available skills is identified for a critical organizational function, this will have to be closed as soon as possible—by appointing an ad interim management and clarifying her/his expected tasks and stated targets.

6.4 Design and Development of Accelerators

Throughout the whole process of the design and set up of a new credit work out unit, a bank should also consider putting in place a system that could help in speeding up the targeted recovery rates of such a platform. As already mentioned, there are a number of strategies, tools and actions that could just allow that, potentially offering the opportunity as well of developing adjacent business that could be offered to the open market and become profitable through time. We refer to such broad set of strategies, tools and actions with the term of "accelerators", as they aim to support the managers in carrying out the credit workout process in a better way—with specific reference to the speediness of the recovery process that should become as "fast and furious" as possible.

Such "accelerators" should be identified, scoped and designed in parallel with the set up of the workout unit and the execution of the crash program, and be closely intertwined and integrated with them: in fact, the value they can add to the recovery of the NPL portfolios comes from the strong interaction with the other components of the work out platform and from the industrial and financial synergies they can achieve. In this section, we analyze two of such potential accelerators, whose role in an active management process will be further explained in a specific chapter later dedicated to the management of NPLs were extended to real estate developers—as both accelerators are connected to real estate underlying. Several of the strategies considered for optimally dealing with troubled credits involve in fact some kind of action on the collateral. In the vast majority of the cases, this is represented by a real estate property, and hence the connection with the real estate sector and its related strategies, tools and actions is easily explained. The accelerators aim therefore at helping a bank to manage underlying assets that are not the main focus of its core business, but that due to the rise of NPLs have nonetheless become a relevant portion of its balance sheet.

While an integrated holistic approach on the topic of active real estate management will later be discussed, this section will focus the analysis on just three of such potential accelerators, e.g. on (1) the real estate agency; on (2) the Real Estate Owned Company (REOCO); and on the (3) active real estate management early warning signals dashboard for a proactive work out. For the three of them, we will now provide a brief explanation of the strategic and industrial rationale for development and a more extended analysis of the operating steps to be followed for doing so.

6.4.1 *Real Estate Agency*

6.4.1.1 The Concept and the Economic Rationale

Developing an internal (e.g. fully owned or at least developed in joint venture with a third party) real estate agency is an attractive opportunity for a bank and for several reasons (see Fig. 6.3). The first one is purely opportunistic, or tactical: as already mentioned, the volume of real estate assets, directly or indirectly owned (via the NPLs with real estate underlying) by the banks is so high, that it makes sense for them to play an active part in this sector, to at least have a better point of view and get more first hand data and market intelligence. The second reason is however more strategic in nature and demand driven: the inherent value, and consequently the potential recovery linked to NPLs is so high that having some competencies and capabilities in this sector is crucial for incrementing the chances of success of the credit work out acting for the bank (in the following discussion, for the sake of simplicity, we will assume this is "captive" to the bank owner of the NPLs assets).

A third potential reason is instead supply driven and based on the way real estate markets are structured. In fact, the real estate sector appears often neither very efficient nor quite competitive and transparent—so that there is actually an opportunity for new players to improve the overall market dynamics, potentially creating a business out of it. This means that besides entering the sector to preserve and defend the value at stake on their "long" positions on NPLs, banks may also consider to have an active, business driven role in the real estate sector to make an extra profit out of it. In fact, they may have some advantages compared to traditional real estate intermediation agencies, especially in countries where the house

	Traditional RE agency		Bank branch	
	Description	Value	Assumption	Value
Revenues	Number of intermediations. - **15-20** (actual market situation); - **25** (liquid market conditions) Average property value: **180-200 k€** Intermediation Fee : **5-6%**	(k€/ year) 140-240 (current) 270 (normal mkt conditions)	Number of intermediations. **10-15** (conservative hyphotesis to take into account lower market penetration of the branch) Average property value: **180-200 k€** Intermediation Fee : **4-5%**	(k€/ year) 70-150
Costs	Agents: 1 HC	~40	Saturation of available resources	✕
	Variable costs: ~ 20% of rev.	30-50	Variable costs	15-30
	Secretary: 1 HC	~30	Saturation of available resources	✕
	Rent: one office with one window	~10	Sinergies with branches	✕
	Utilities (energy, internet, phone, ...)	~6	Sinergies with branches	✕
	Advertsing (specialized websites, ...)	12-15	Necessary expense	12-15
Margin		**10-90**		**40-100**

Fig. 6.3 The real estate agency business for a bank's branch. Impact of the real estate agency versus traditional branch—cost analysis. *Source* Internal analysis

market is less transparent and hence many transactions are carried out among private counterparties rather than through real estate agencies (and, in most cases, the service offered by the traditional agencies is perceived as rather poor). In these markets, the limited recourse to agencies is usually explained by a combination of excessively high fees, the scarcity of the offer available both in terms of properties and additional services, and by the general distrust towards those agencies—often acting in less than transparent ways.

A bank could act on most of those factors and become a valid alternative to a real estate agency.

For what concerns its fees, the commission based pricing adopted by the bank could potentially be slightly more aggressive than the rest of the market (e.g. target lower fees per Euro of transaction) because the bank would be able to leverage most of its fixed costs distribution structure and make up with an extra margin coming from its traditional lending activity (plus, potentially, from the cross selling of other related P&C insurance products). In fact, a bank could draw most of the human resources needed for running the agency from its unsaturated work capacity, and use its own branches as points of sale. Also the cost of utilities would be reduced thanks to the synergies with the branches. The newly set up real estate agency unit of the bank would then obviously incur in incremental advertising and communication costs—mostly variable; but also on this front the bank would be able to leverage better the effects coming from any single Euro spent—aimed in any case at reaching and nurturing its current and prospect client base, and as a part of a consistent relationship building effort which would transcend the otherwise quite narrow "financial" need to address other important and more extensive needs, such as the "housing" one.

On the side of the sourcing process of the properties to be sold, a bank could effectively exploit the scale of its lending business and leverage further the scope of its branch network, and then try to involve a significant portion of its clients' properties in the intermediation business of the agency.

On the positive side, the issue of mistrust that seems to affect the real estate agency sector could be at least partially addressed by the fact that the client already has a long term relationship with the bank and values in a better way the "brand name" of a bank in terms of "trust" and "reliability".

By developing a well designed real estate agency offering, a bank could hence become a strong player in a market that is for most European Countries currently neither very efficient nor at scale.

6.4.1.2 The Management of a Real Estate Agency

The management of a real estate agency initiative has also relevant implication on the management of NPLs as well. As already explained in a previous chapter (in our discussion on the credit lifecycle), even if it detects the signs of some credit deterioration, at an early stage a bank can only use its moral suasion to protect its interests. However, if the bank has a significant leading presence in the real estate market, it may have greater chances of inducing its clients to take corrective actions on their positions, because it is in the best situation to assist them in reducing their risk, facilitating the sale or utilization of their properties in an effective and efficient way.

One of the main areas of concern is in fact related to the optimization of the value of the collateral. If this is a "buy to rent" kind of property, the bank could for example help its lending counterpart in maximizing the income she/he gets from it by promoting the asset in the renting market. On one side, the bank could offer to leverage its unique access to potential end users, helping the debtor in getting the more favorable renting conditions and reducing its time to market of the asset; on the other side, it could offer lower transaction fees than other traditional real estate agents in the market. Both effects would increase the net income for its customer and hence reduce his probability of default on the loan already provided by the bank. Moreover, the bank would have more and better information on the actual use and income related to the property reducing the chances that it loses its value (a flat being used is usually better kept than an unused one).

Given this clear economic rationale for developing a real estate agency business, a bank should consider starting this new venture by carrying out a feasibility study to make sure that in its specific situation the business and operational set up of the project are sufficiently strong to justify it.

If the study justifies and reinforces the decision to develop the agency, the bank would have then to decide what is the best way to design it and which kind of legal, organizational and IT & operations systems to put in place, in order to make it work as an effective accelerator in support of the credit workout process—e.g. not just as a new business per se, but as an integrated component to its overall recovery strategy on its NPL portfolios. In this regard, there are several actions to undertake before actually considering the launch of a pilot. They are summarized in the following paragraphs.

6.4.1.3 The Real Estate Agency Structure and Set Up

The very first step on this initiative is usually focused on the choice of the optimal legal setup for the new company, taking into account the regulatory requirements that may vary across different jurisdictions. Depending on the role that the agency has in the overall business of the bank, the form chosen can be different, and consequently the documentation and red taping required can be more or less heavy. Usually, this process will take a few months due to the legal procedures required.

In this phase, the bank should also take some critical decisions, and specifically it should define the concept and the branding strategy and develop a marketing plan for the launch of the real estate agency business. The choice of the brand name is not as trivial as it would appear at first sight, given few inherent trade offs to consider: on one side a bank may want to exploit the potential of its brand awareness by naming the agency after its own name—the eponymous brand could be for example "bank ABC real estate agency"; on the other side, it has to make sure that the final structure is consistent with its banking strategy, not diluting its core brand and business perception and minimizing the potential reputational risks. Considerations of this sort may impact the final choice as to what extent to make a direct link between the new real estate agency and the bank.

Once this kind of communication and marketing elements of the vision have been clarified, the bank should then address the working requirements of the new company, providing it with both the human capital and the physical and IT infrastructure it requires for becoming fully operational. In practical terms, this means identifying the branches where to set up a real estate agency point of sales, either as dedicated space, corner point or just as temporary exposition with advertisements. It also means setting up a managerial team and a network of real estate agents that can run the agency and develop and execute the business. As already mentioned, the bank's competitiveness in the real estate sector should derive from the use of its unsaturated capacity in terms of personnel and unutilized distribution network space (plus, of course, the leverage of its mortgage lending, payments and home insurance offerings). In any case, some degree of "conversion costs" of such resources should be considered as minimum requirement, in order to make them adequate to the new purpose they will be devoted to. For the personnel, after the initial gap analysis phase, the bank should therefore proceed with the set up of the training program (as both formal and on the job training) that would make the resources provided actually suited for performing the activities.

In fact, the people involved in the agency will likely need different kinds of business profiles, due to the variety of activities that the agency could perform. The operating team should end up being made of real estate agency consultants that can be either internal or external and of managers, ranging from sales managers responsible for local areas to managers in charge of the coordinating and supporting activities. The complexity of the tasks required might make identifying a project management officer, who can supervise the whole operation, necessary. The bank could also consider hiring "ad interim" managers that could support the project through its different phases.

As for the bank's branches, some kind of refurbishing and restructuring of the work space should be planned as well, to make the place as suitable as possible to the agency business (e.g. the branch should be accessible for longer hours and on Saturday, and without the cumbersome security check points to get in and out). Once the basic infrastructure is put in place, the next phase will consist in making the market aware of the existence of the new real estate agency business performed by the bank. The marketing process should be initiated at an early stage, because it will take some time in order to start having some effects in the market: building brand awareness is in fact crucial for the success of the agency and considerable effort should be dedicated to this phase. Due to the specificity of the service offered, the bank could also want to use a below the line marketing strategy, e.g. having sales agents advertising the new agency directly at branch level, in order to target its existing customers. To some extent, it may also resort to external marketing and communication support functions, using "broad band" media to reach out non clients as well.

At this stage, the bank should also start planning the launch of a pilot, initially on a limited (but statistically representative) number of branches. Moreover, it should also consider setting up a dedicated web site for the digital promotion of the new offering—it could just engage with some real estate existing portals that are usually available for white labelling their own platform for a minimal fee. Once the set up phase has been completed, the real estate agency will start acquiring mandates to sell real estate properties: getting sales mandates and then closing transactions with potential buyers will constitute the chore of its activities and produce the bulk of its future revenues.

6.4.2 *REOCO*

6.4.2.1 The Concept and Its Economic Rationale

As explained, a bank owned real estate agency has the potential to achieve significant cost synergies and become a competitor in the real estate intermediation market. This may be relevant when talking about non performing loans but also sub performing ones. For this last case, the agency can contribute to the improvement of the situation of distressed debtors who derive part of their income from real estate assets, or whose position is collateralized by a real estate property. Despite the benefits it provides, setting up a real estate agency cannot however be considered a necessary and sufficient solution for a bank who aims at becoming a truly active workout manager. Indeed, the strong interconnectedness between the real estate market and the non performing loans one, suggests that a bank could undertake more extensive action in this sector.

In this sense, a Real Estate Owned Company (REOCO) represents a further step in the right direction, in a complementary way with the previous initiative of setting up an agency.

A REOCO is a company that is specifically designed to acquire real estate assets in the competitive bidding process that aims for the final sale of the collateral underlying the NPL. Nevertheless, its involvement in the process is not limited to the acquisition of the asset, but it may extends over the whole duration of the recovery activity: in fact, besides acquiring them, the REOCO is also responsible for actively managing the real estate assets, getting some yield whilst it owns them and then driving the following sale process, with a view of maximizing their exit value.

During the acquisition phase, the REOCO carries out its activities since the very beginning of the asset sale process. In fact, it participates to court procedures regarding the forced sale of real estate assets and it is involved in bankruptcy agreements which may concern the sale of real estate assets; in this way, it should be able to negotiate better terms and conditions using the wealth of information it has on the asset (being owned by the lender) and in some case its bargaining power.

Besides the fact that it takes an active part in the legal process, the REOCO truly contributes to the real estate assets value maximization in a way that differs depending on whether the NPLs connected with the assets are captive or non captive (see Fig. 6.4). In the case of non captive NPLs (loans that are not owned by the bank that is parent company to the REOCO), the portfolios can be segmented into different categories and with a high degree of granularity. This segmentation allows to the bank to provide value added services to target clients, e.g. smaller financial institutions, institutional investors but also small businesses and private

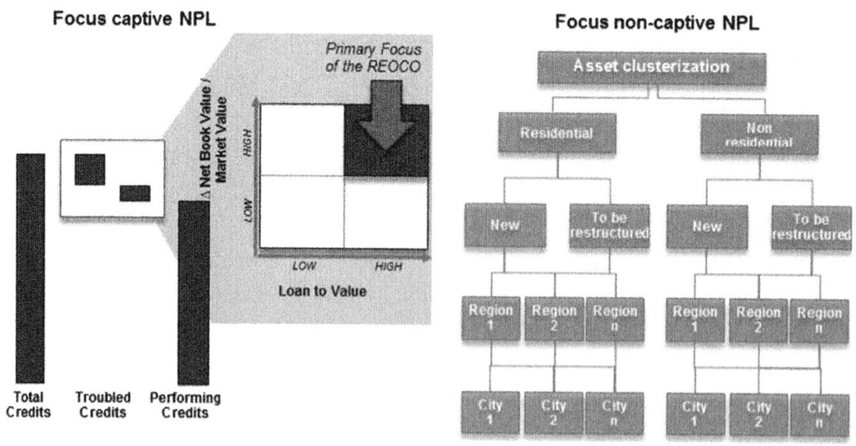

Fig. 6.4 Prioritizing the opportunities for recovery REOCO feasibility study. *Source* Internal analysis

clients, with a view of developing this activity into a potentially new revenues generating business opportunity.

In the case of captive NPL portfolios, the REOCO could also perform value added services, and not for a fee but just as part of the bank's value preserving strategy, focusing its range of interventions on the portion of the portfolio that shows a higher loan to value and a greater gap in terms of difference between market and book value, as the opportunities for recover are bigger.

6.4.2.2 The Management of a REOCO

The REOCO usually participates to both public and private auctions aimed at the disposal of the collateral of a defaulted debt. Acting as a specialized player in the bidding process, the REOCO can enhance the competitive environment, the transparency and publicity of the auction process and achieve several benefits (see Fig. 6.5). Potentially, there are two completely different strategies that can be adopted. On one side, the REOCO may not be interested in acquiring the assets, but it may still participate to the auction in order to create pressure on the other bidders so as to move upward the price of the collateral. By doing so, the value of the real estate asset would be maximized, and consequently the net value recovered from the NPLs would increase. In this way, a bank is hence able avoid that the asset gets sold at prices that do not reflect at all the market situation (from one auction process to the other, the typical discount on the starting price is 20 % circa). A second, apparently different but in reality quite complementary approach could instead involve competing in the auction to acquire the asset at the lowest possible price to realize a profit on its later resale.

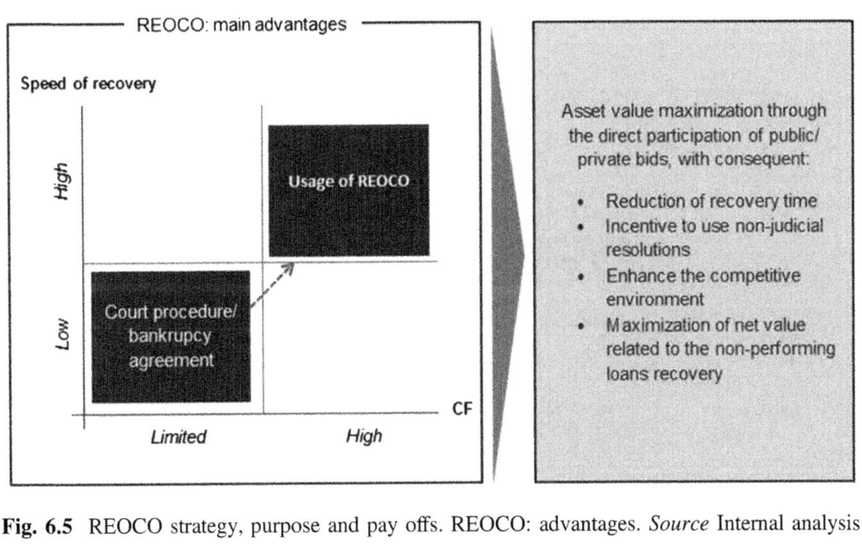

Fig. 6.5 REOCO strategy, purpose and pay offs. REOCO: advantages. *Source* Internal analysis

While the first strategy provides immediate, although somewhat limited, benefits for the bank, the second is more long term oriented, but opens to the possibility of creating greater value, after the full benefits linked to the active management of the assets are completely realized. In fact, benefits do not come from an immediate recovery on the collateral, but from the added value that the REOCO can bring to the asset. This is why the role of the REOCO extends beyond a simple acquisition vehicle, and encompasses an active management follow up phase as well.

Once it has acquired the assets, the REOCO should coordinate and execute (either directly or through outsourcing) a series of activities which could include, for example, the facility, property management and asset management as already defined in the previous chapter. It is nonetheless worthwhile to remind that those activities can range in terms of impact and value added to the different assets (see Fig. 6.6). On one side, facility management simply aims at keeping the value of properties intact by optimizing the costs for maintaining them functioning and in good order. If the REOCO does not envisage significant ameliorating actions beyond maintenance, its role in the auction should probably be limited to the first strategy discussed above (driving the price of the collateral up as much as possible). On the other hand, asset management has a strategic target and it aims at increasing the "to be" value of the assets until it reaches a level in line with that of their Highest and Best Available Use (H-BAU). This situation offers greater opportunities to add value beyond the market level, so that in this case the REOCO should evaluate the option of making a competitive bid to acquire the asset. The decision

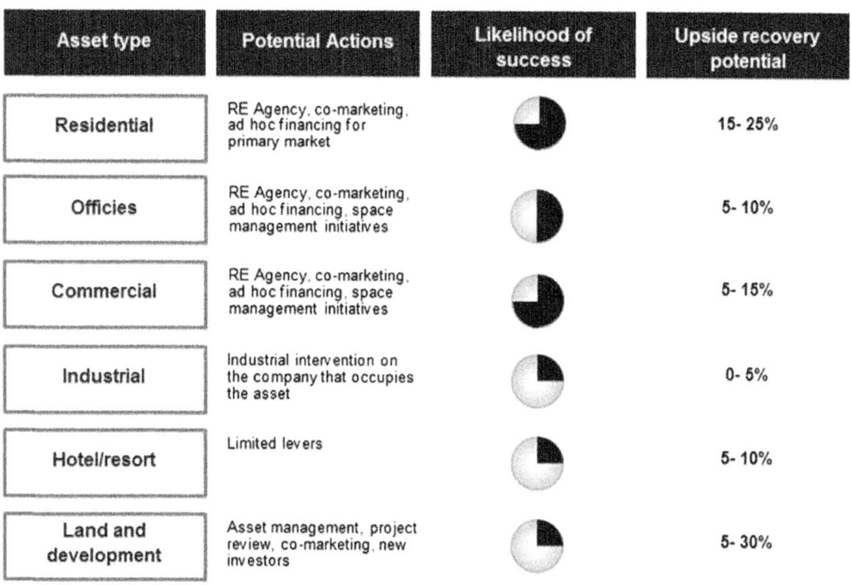

Fig. 6.6 Real estate assets tipologies and potential recovery Features of assets and likelihood of success. *Source* Internal analysis

should obviously be made also taking into account the likelihood of success of the corrective actions and their upside potential, whose value depends mainly on the features of the assets bought. Figure 6.6 exemplifies this issue; for example, actions on commercial and residential properties have a good balance between chances of success and upside potential, while land and development projects are much riskier both because the chances of success are lower and because the recovery level is much more volatile.

Through a proper active management approach, the REOCO can increase the value of the assets; the last stage of the process is therefore aimed at capturing such added value by choosing and implementing an optimal exit (sale) strategy. This should be carried out by using a mix of distribution channels: web and digital marketplaces, corporate and retail agents (either national or local) and financial transactions advisors for major properties. A bank that has already other accelerators in place, and specifically one that has implemented a real estate agency, would have a clear advantage, as it could use its own agency as the main distribution channel. Even if it does not own a real estate agency, a bank could consider using its branches as a key channel for the sale of real estate assets, both repossessed and not. It could also eventually resort to financial incentives (e.g. cheaper rates on the banks mortgages), if needed, to stimulate potential buyers (see Fig. 6.7). The different recovery strategies as shown above could be executed in line with the potential upside of the asset and with its need of cash, as illustrated in Fig. 6.7

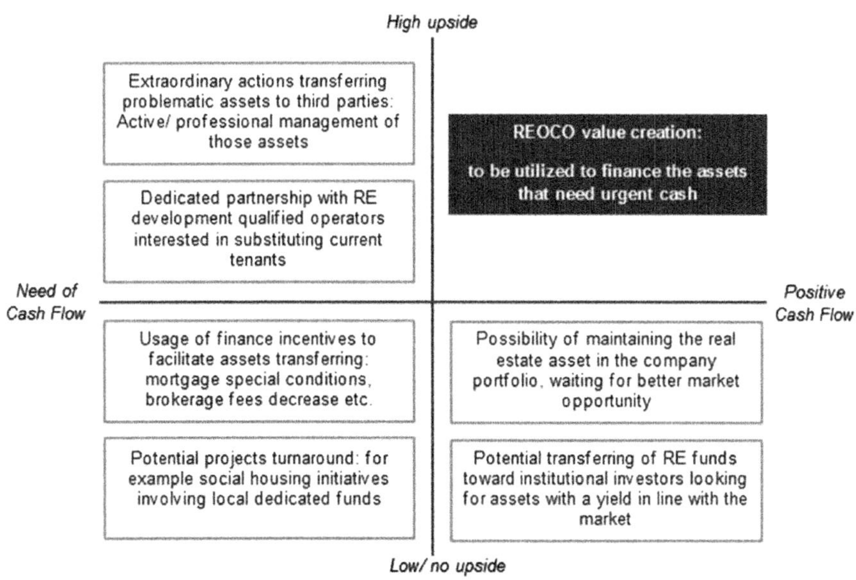

Fig. 6.7 A potential frame for analysis REOCO: different strategies. *Source* Internal analysis

6.4.2.3 The REOCO Structure and Its Set Up

As explained, a REOCO can be an effective accelerator because it can speed up and optimize the recovery process of NPLs. This section aims then at identifying the most critical areas that have to be considered when setting up its structure. A bank should initially consider developing a feasibility study, which can be articulated under four dimensions. The first would regard some technical aspects, in order to define a clear initial perimeter for the operational activity of the REOCO, identifying which loans it will be responsible for following the auction process. The cutoff point may be specified on the basis of several aspects, for example the segment, kind, status, location, vintage, monetary amount, gap between market and book value, market demand and many other dimensions. The potential upsides and critical areas for the REOCO that each of the resulting perimeters of activity can lead to, have then to be evaluated through simulations. Once the perimeter has been identified, clear indications should be given on how to aggregate selected NPLs for procedural and organizational purposes. This should allow the identification of which of the clusters deriving from the combination of the different dimensions should be prioritized. The bank should then evaluate how to develop an integrated database to collect the loans' relevant information and which are the best IT solutions for managing an integrated REOCO. In this sense, it is particularly important to make sure that the data collected are reliable, for example by checking that the assessed valuation of the real estate property is reasonable. Further on, the feasibility and convenience of different legal and fiscal set ups has to be evaluated, possibly resorting to the advice of lawyers with experience in the real estate sector. Lastly, the bank has to examine whether there exist operational or reputational risks, either affecting the characteristic activities in a specific way, or impacting on the holistic, integrated business vision as a whole. If there are concerns in this respect, the bank has to take action to solve any potential conflict of interest.

The second dimension to analyze is related to the business model of the REOCO. Once the principal activities and capabilities required are identified, it is necessary to determine to what extent they should be internalized. Depending on the respective economic convenience, different activities could be managed in house, outsourced, or developed with the help of a strategic partner. This decision also affects the economics underlying the REOCO, which could act as a pure servicer for the bank and stand as a cost center or carry out transactions with third parties as well. The relationship with external agents, either corporate or retail, is particularly important in the case in which the REOCO offers also additional value added services besides just focusing on its core activity. Those could be closely related or complementary to the main business and can range from facility, property and asset management to ideating and structuring complex loans portfolios for resale. Depending on the kind of activities the REOCO plans to perform, different governance models and capital structure may be appropriate. On one extreme the bank may have full ownership, on the other it may consider developing a joint venture with a financial sponsor or other commercial banks in order to have third parties participating to the equity capital of the company.

The third area to consider in the REOCO feasibility study is connected with the operating structure. From an organizational perspective it is necessary to initially identify the macrostructure and then define the optimal level of the targets for each unit or function, taking into account the degree of in or outsourcing for each of them. Moreover, for each activity there should be clear indications on which are the core families of competencies (skills, experience and behavior) required to perform it. The REOCO should also have internal macro processes in order to coordinate this with the other divisions of the bank and with external counterparties. It should also define the guidelines that can help creating an incentive system for both its "service" and its "profit" activities. This can be done by identifying drivers of both financial and industrial nature to evaluate the performance and to handle the relationships with third parties through different service level agreements. For what concerns human resources, it is clear that if the workforce of the REOCO is partially or mostly made up of people that were previously employed in the bank, a significant conversion and training program should be set in place in order to make employees more knowledgeable on the real estate business. The program should cover different topics and include real estate valuation and management, structured finance, credit valuation and recovery and other legal and fiscal background knowledge that could prove useful when participating to the liquidation procedures.

The final area of action in the feasibility study is dedicated to developing a business case and a master plan for the realization of the REOCO. First, it is essential to determine the economic convenience of the project by comparing the gain in the net present value that the new activity can bring to the bank compared to the status quo. This is a crucial activity, because the result will determine whether the REOCO is actually a viable solution or whether the bank would be better served by keeping its "as is" structure or using third parties REOCOs. In order to estimate the net present value of the project, the bank should define its expected returns, its fixed and variable costs and investment plans under different business models and risk appetite scenarios. It should prepare different prospective income statements depending on whether the REOCO operates as a service (e.g. pure cost) center or as a profit center, since the elements to analyze are different for the two models. In the first case, the bank should consider different hypotheses on the value at which the repossessed assets can be booked, and their cost of funding, regulatory impact, capital expenses required and net income expected. In the case in which the REOCO is a profit center, the bank should estimate which services it would offer to third parties and what the related fees could be. If the economic convenience test is passed, a master plan for the set up and start up of the REOCO activities can then be developed. This should contain information of legal, fiscal and regulatory nature as well as details about the timing, costs and interrelations among the actors of the project.

6.4.3 *Active Real Estate Management (AREM)*

6.4.3.1 The Idea, the Setup and the Structure

In order to set up an "active real estate management" (AREM) dashboard, some critical elements must be carefully addressed. As already mentioned, the function of an AREM dashboard relies on the identification of particular situations that could be moving towards a sub performing status. For this purpose, the bank has to update and check the real estate database that it has previously built up and define all the fields that are required and most critical. Most importantly, it has to verify the consistency of the information reported and, if it has not done it already, it must complete and organize all the missing data about the characteristics of the collateral or of all other kind of guarantees. The goal is to create a unique database that is reliable and exhaustive.

After having collected and arranged the data available, the bank has then to design a dashboard aimed at monitoring the status and situation of the collateral assets through a limited but meaningful set of industrial and financial key performance indicators (KPIs—or Early Warning Signals—EWS). On this basis, the bank has to test the statistical correlation and the predictive capability of the KPI that has initially identified: this could be done through back testing and stress testing. The dashboard could also include KPIs concerning operational and reputational risks, built using a mix of quantitative and qualitative information via sampling and judgemental analysis. The bank has then to identify the most critical situations that require some prioritized action, and operate on them through "ad hoc" crash programs, so that the recovered value is maximized in the short run. Standard intervention processes have to be defined as well: each process entailing any kind of proactive management has to refer to a specific kind of NPls, previously identified through clusters. Once it has defined the standard and extraordinary actions that have to be taken, the bank has to set the internal structures and responsibilities necessary to implement the AREM approach.

Chapter 7
Managing Competitively NPL Portfolios and Third Party Servicers

Abstract Credit work out excellence is increasingly built on a superior management of the underlying collateral of the troubled assets—be it a real estate asset backing a mortgage or an equipment tied to a leasing contract, or the borrowing company itself. In order to develop an active approach to underlying collaterals active management, a proper data base need to be build and maintained through time. Then, a comprehensive dashboard can be develop to highlight traditional and non traditional approaches to preserve and maximize the assets market value and help in realizing their best value, given the chosen time horizon and sales strategy. The maximum "to be" value and best exit strategy can be defined based on a number of valuation analysis and scenario simulations that consider different recovery costs, speed to market and operational/reputational risks.

Keywords Collaterals active management · Credit workout excellence · Data assessment · Monitoring and evaluation · Scenario analysis · Strategy implementation

7.1 Managing Competitively NPL Portfolios

In the previous chapters we have analyzed the different designs that could be considered to set up a credit workout unit and explained the steps involved in developing an active, holistic one. Hopefully, the analysis has shown that actively managing NPL portfolios can evolve from being a pure defensive strategy to becoming a bigger source of value recovery and even—potentially—a new source of opportunities for the launch of new revenues producing business activities for the bank. Obviously, unlocking this potential is not cost and risk free, and, as seen in the previous chapter, creating a workout unit is a quite complex process, which requires a great deal of effort and commitment, both in terms of time and resources spent. Before undertaking such commitment a bank has therefore to evaluate

C. Scardovi, *Holistic Active Management of Non-Performing Loans*,
DOI 10.1007/978-3-319-25363-3_7

whether it has the right set of capabilities that make it possible for it to become an "alpha player", capable to outplay third parties in terms of recovery effectiveness.

A realistic analysis of whether the value that can be extracted by managing portfolios internally is the best option from an economic point of view is hence needed. This value should always be compared with what can be achieved through any other alternative strategy, in order to determine the best course of action. Assessing how much a credit is worth under different scenarios, e.g. ending up being managed by different parties is hence crucial. This is why in this chapter we take a step back and explain how to fully evaluate a NPLs portfolio and under different scenarios, before moving again to the analysis of best recovery strategies (whether done internally or outsourced).

7.2 An Approach to Credit Workout Excellence

It not easy to identify the "true" intrinsic value for a portfolio of NPLs. On one side, it is clear that the amount they were initially accounted for in the balance sheet of the originating bank is nomore reliable. At the same time the market value of those loans is most probably quite below their real value, since they are seen as "bad" debts. Being these loans already on default, their value is not connected to anything but the expected recovery on them. However, the estimation of such a recovery rate through time is not an easy process. Therefore, we have identified the three steps that a bank could follow in order to come out with a valuation for the NPL portfolios that is as much realistic as possible (see Fig. 7.1). The assessment of an NPL portfolio database, identified as first step, aims at having a clear and organized overview of the loans to be managed and consequently at having a base over which to value them and then design a workout strategy. The organization of a structured database has become particularly crucial nowadays as the amount of NPLs has been increasing exponentially, with its huge variety of contracts characteristics and peculiarities. The construction of an NPL database begins therefore with the appraisal of the quality and subsequent review of the information currently available on the NPLs and on their underlying collateral assets.

It is important to underline that the value of the collateral assets is an extremely crucial element for the assessment of the whole NPL portfolio, since the recovered value often comes just from it. More precisely, the collateral fair value and potential market value have to be verified through an analysis of second opinions for any single specific category of real estate assets. On the other side, all the industrial and financial information for both the real estate and for the other kind of collateral assets has to be collected. In the case of leasing equipment, the underlying asset may vary a lot and therefore the process of categorization and valuation can become pretty unreliable and difficult.

When all the necessary information has then been collected, the bank is ready to set a price to the NPLs portfolio and to consequentially implement a credit workout strategy based on that. As we will explain in more detail later, the value of a

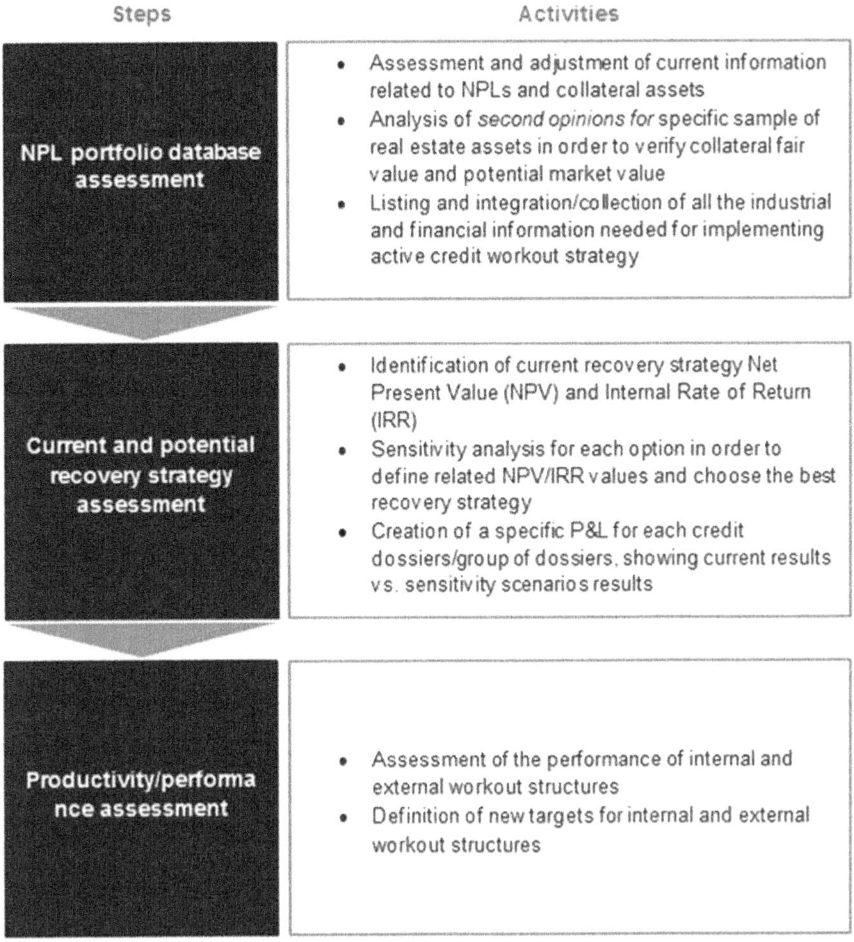

Fig. 7.1 An active credit work out dashboard. *Source* Own illustration based on internal analysis

portfolio is firstly estimated as an "as is", for its "ceteris paribus" embedded value, and then for its "to be", that is when are taken into account all the possible active and holistic actions that would increase and optimize its value through time.

The assessed value is then analyzed in order to find the optimal way to deal with such portfolio. The choice of the recovery strategy is based on the calculation and analysis of two key parameters that are the Net Present Value (NPV) and the Internal Rate of Return (IRR) associated with the "long" position that the bank has on the NPL portfolio. Of course, the bank aims at the maximization of both of them in order to realize the maximum value from its workout strategy. For each single dossier or group of NPLs that has been identified, the bank has therefore to design a different and targeted potential recovery strategy: it is important that the strategy identified for each cluster of NPLs is matching its specific characteristics, thus addressing them in the best possible way. After the initial calculation and analysis of the NPV and IRR for each cluster, the bank has then to implement a sensitivity analysis in order to identify a feasible range of performance values that would help tailor the best recovery strategy if some of the endogenous or exogenous conditions will change through time. As a last step, the analysis has to define a profit and loss target for each category of NPLs, comparing actual results with the forecasts of the sensitivity analysis.

Once determined the best recovery strategy for any single NPL portfolio and the potential optimal value from recovery, the bank is in a better position to negotiate and analyse the performance expected and then realized by external collection servicers and credit workout structures.

7.3 NPL Portfolios Database Assessment

The first step for the design, development, and full implementation of a "holistic and active" workout dashboard for the management of nplS entails the collection of the required (necessary and sufficient) information. In particular, the information needed to develop an optimal dashboard for monitoring, controlling and dynamic planning is of great importance and must be fully understood and prioritized. A complete and updated database would give the bank all the right information needed to assess the value of its NPLs in its balance sheet, and provide the critical information on the basis of which define and manage its best recovery strategy (see Fig. 7.2). First of all, it is important to source and store the relevant data on the key attributes of the credit product and of its collateral. These kind of information may include the ticket size of each loan, the number and frequency of its payments, the length of the contract etc. The terms and conditions usually associated with the loan contract should also be selectively identified and stored, as they will give suggestions on the likelihood of a recovery. Also the credit history, for example in terms of the number of payments made over the total payment requested or the average delay in payments, should be sourced and stored.

The end customer characteristics represent an important set of data as well. The portfolio of a bank is rightfully composed of exposures to many different creditors. It is necessary therefore to identify the customer profiles and segments. A macro segmentation is the one dividing exposures towards retail clients—families, individuals and very small businesses (mortgage loans, consumer loans etc.) or towards corporates. This set of info must then include such attributes as the size of the counterpart, the location in which it operates and the industry or industries in which it is active. Moreover, it must be assessed if a customer has multiple relationships with the bank, and what kind of business relationships they are (often, they do not concern just the credit side of the banking business, but may include payments and transactions services, asset management, private banking etc.). The strength and length of the bank's relationship with a certain customer can then greatly influence the bank's perception about the potential recovery of a contract and influence its

DB Information	Main mistakes
SURFACE	• No Data • Data not correlated to economic value (e.g. commercial value for shops, ...) • Mistakes in data entry • Data not correlated to asset destination (e.g. one data comprehensive of core and not core assets – gardens, boxes, ...)
VALUE	• Obsolete value (e.g. old estimation never updates • Mistakes in data entry • Evaluation criteria not coherent with asset destination (e.g. construction costs to estimate open market value) • Evaluation scope not coherent with open market value definition (e.g. insurance scope) • Evaluation based on wrong/incomplete input data
TECHNICAL-LEGAL ASSESSMENT	• Wrong cadastral data (e.g. address, maps, ...) • Incomplete documentation (e.g. energetic certification) • Limited highlighting of third parties rights on the asset (e.g. mortgages, ...) • Wrong/missing indication on several economic bulks (e.g. rents, income, ...) • Wrong indication of the destination of the asset
PHYSICAL IDENTIFICATION	• Wrong maintenance status • No photographic documentation • No indication of detrimental events (e.g. blaze, water damage, ...) • Not updated documentation (e.g. presence of lofts not indicated on the official map, ...)

Fig. 7.2 A checklist on the reliability of data bases. Examples of most frequent mistakes found on banks databases. *Source* Internal analysis

credit work out approach, given the greater amount of information and statistics available and the greater negotiating power it could command (or the commercial caveats it will have to consider)—usually the same underwriting rules and pricing strategy applied to a certain customer might change according to the length of his relationship with the bank and the cross selling of products achieved.

The acquisition channel (the distribution channel that originated the sale of the loan and through which the relationship with the client has been mainly managed) represents a third area of data that has to be carefully assessed. In particular, a contract could be stipulated either through a local or regional relationship manager, directly at a bank's branch, or through external, third party agents, such as a mortgage broker, or via internet or a call center. Ideally, for each channel should be analysed the split of customers acquired, the geographical distribution reached and the effectiveness and efficacy of past credit approval processes. The ones above mentioned are just a summary of all the data that have to be collected by a bank in order to build up and run a credit workout database. Ideally, all the information that can allow a useful categorization and organization of NPL portfolios must be included. In practice, several mistakes and missing or misleading information can usually be found in databases. Those errors are mainly related to a wrong valuation of the collateral assets. When taking into consideration NPLs, it is therefore paramount to make sure that all the main information on collateral assets are captured and reliable (avoiding the typical mistakes enlisted below), since they drive most of the actual recoverable value.

7.4 Portfolio Valuation and Recovery Strategy Implementation

The value of each portfolio has to be assessed by taking into account two different dimensions (see Fig. 7.3). Under an "as is" valuation, what matters most is the embedded value of the portfolio, assuming a "ceteris paribus" approach: determining this is important because it constitutes a more or less objective starting point for the following decisions. Under a "to be" valuation framework instead, a bank

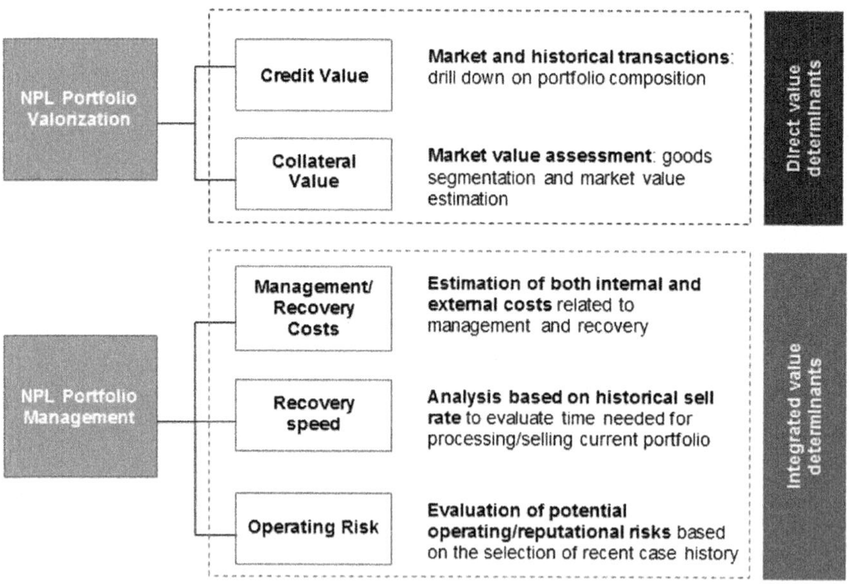

Fig. 7.3 Breaking down portfolio value creation opportunities. Breaking down value creation opportunities. *Source* Internal analysis

has to evaluate what the portfolio could be worth after the workout process. This means taking into account what it could potentially achieve through its holistic and active management. It is important to notice that both components are essential and that, while estimating the "to be" value is certainly more complex, enough attention should be dedicated to the "as is" valuation as well. In fact, intrinsic value should not be considered simply under a "static" dimension: what matters is not only the size, but also the "timing" of the credit. In the next section, this concept will be further clarified, but since now it should be clear that the analysis is not as straightforward as it may initially seem. Time plays an even more relevant role on the value components coming from portfolio management, and this helps understanding why the focus of NPLs recovery is on achieving the maximum speed in the process by adopting a "fast and furious" approach.

7.5 The "as is" Value

When considering the "as is" value, there are two different components that play a role in the NPL valuation, namely, the value of the credit and the value of the collateral (see Fig. 7.4).

The reason why they must be analyzed separately is that the first part pertains to what a bank could still get under a normal repayment scenario (in a subperforming scenario, the bank is likely to recover from it just a portion of the principal outstanding), while the second has a great importance since it was originally set up to

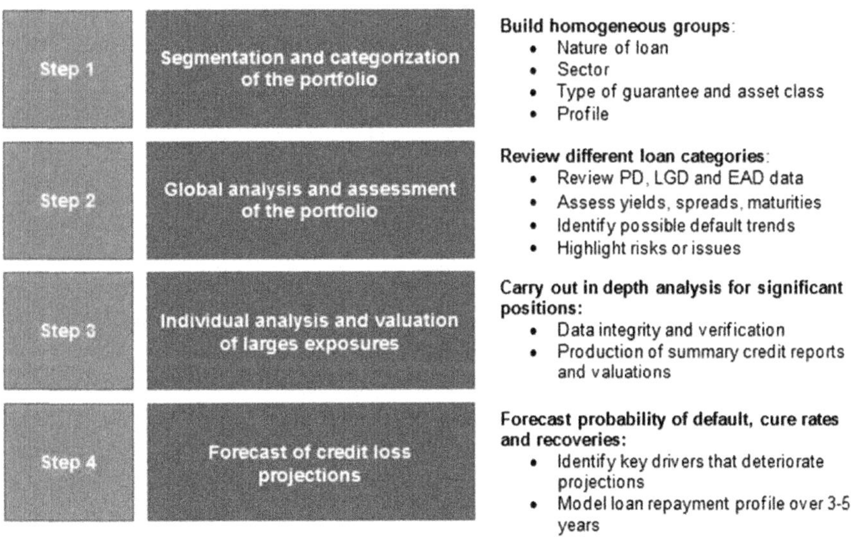

Fig. 7.4 NPL valuation: a dynamic approach. Optimal approach for assessing credit value. *Source* Internal analysis

ensure the best recovery in case of default. When assessing the value of the credit, as shown in Fig. 7.4, there are four key steps to undertake.

The first step consists in identifying the main drivers that impact on the credit value in broader terms. The main drivers are then used to segment and categorize the portfolios on the basis of homogeneous characteristics. The key elements to be considered for the analysis are similar to those that were discussed when talking about portfolio clusterization, and indeed the logic behind the segmentation process is the same: each loan has to be organized into a group of similar loans. Its value can then be inferred by looking at what these similar loans have experienced, on the assumption that it will behave in the same fashion. Some important variables for segmentation that were already discussed are the ticket size, the legal status of the debtor, the presence of third party guarantees and the vintage. In this section we want to further point out how all these aspects have to be considered under a dynamic dimension: in fact, NPLs that appear similar under a static point of view, may have very different recovery values when considering their dynamic dimension through time as well, and it is therefore important that their differences be accounted for in order to categorize them in the right group. For example, it is clear that two loans, given the same "size" in terms of book value, should be treated very differently depending on whether the amount reported is the residual of a much larger exposure for which the greatest portion has been paid down over the full outstanding initial debt. Moreover, possible interrelations among driving factors have to be considered as well. For example, it is not possible to categorize a loan based on its maturity without taking into account the legal status of the debtor as well. In fact, this has an important impact on the recovery perspective, and hence values that may seem alarming under some conditions need not be considered so under other circumstances. For example, liquidation procedures may take very long, and hence a loan that has been classified as NPL for several years may still have some recovery potential if some judicial action has been taken. On the other hand, recovery chances for a long time expired loan for which no repossessing procedure has been initiated are limited. Further elements to be considered for segmentation are summarized below (Fig. 7.5).

The reason for considering these criteria is that for each of them it is then possible to evaluate parameters that may be relevant for credit valuation, by using both current and historical data. In this sense, the second step in portfolio valuation consists in assessing yields, spreads and amortization rates for each different loan cohort and category. Moreover, for each of these groups, a bank should review collections, charges, exposures, provisions, default rates and loss given default data. Finally it should identify restructured, rescheduled and refinanced loans. Besides allowing to collect data that can be used at a later valuation stage in a logical and meaningful way, a segmented structure allows the identification of potential arrears and default trends in each cluster, as it may help highlighting evident risks or issues, both past and future. The analysis has relevant implications and this is why it has to be conducted under a dynamic perspective, taking into account both the current and historical performances of the portfolios, together with the possible more lax credit

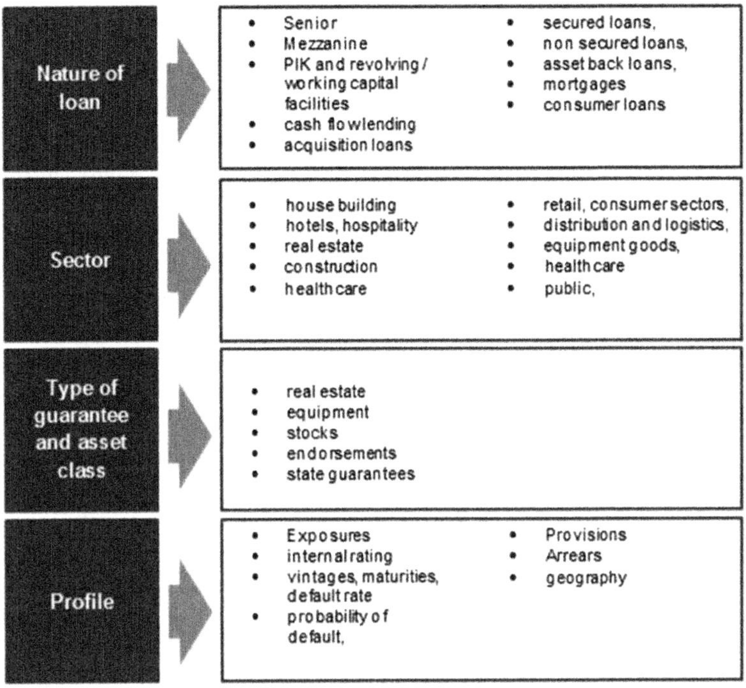

Fig. 7.5 Criteria to approach segmentation. *Source* Internal analysis

and underwriting policies that could have characterized the credit policies of past times.

When possible and appropriate, it may also be useful to resort to benchmarks (e.g. analysis of peers' portfolios and past performances of securitizations, including international experiences). Finally, in order to have a more comprehensive picture, a brief perspective on the region economic, real estate and SME sector context, both current and expected, should also be considered. The whole analysis should then be carried out firstly at a global level, and then applied to each portfolio. After this first tow sets of valuation, the third step consists in moving to an individual analysis: each portfolio should be broken down into their single exposures, and the largest among them should be valuated separately. For the selected loans, the bank has to evaluate the recoverable exposures, conducting a detailed analysis on the files' documentation, using all relevant and available information. The aim of this analysis carried out to generate a forecast of credit loss projections. The final step consists then in modelling the extent to which loans may be repaid in a certain time horizon. On one side, this requires estimating a series of parameters relevant for computing the expected loss, such as the probability of default, the exposure at default and the loss given default; on the other side, it requires taking into consideration other factors as well, such as the quality of the information related to the borrower or to the initiatives underway that may impact the value of the portfolio.

The modeling assumptions differ on the basis of sector, type of loan and historical data and this allows a more accurate projection. It is necessary to stress once more that what really matters is the expected recovery value over time: in this sense the forecast should be as precise as possible also in terms of timing, in order to make it possible to correctly account for discounting and time value.

In any case, the credit component constitutes only one face of the "as is" value. The second relevant element to consider for portfolio valorization is in fact represented by its collateral value. As already stressed in the previous chapters, monitoring and measuring the collateral correctly is fundamental, because it is what the bank will be left with in case the borrower ends up being unable to repay. There are several factors that need to be considered in order to carry out a proper valuation. Specifically, the marketability of collateral depends on its actual market value, the status of the company which is currently using it, its transfer costs, the number of potential buyers and their geographical location. These dimensions are reported and briefly analyzed in Fig. 7.6.

The most important aspect to consider when valuing collateral is certainly the category to which the asset belongs. In fact, assets of different kinds have very different profiles, both in terms of how easy they are to market and of how fast they loose value. These aspects need to be carefully analyzed, since when a bank becomes the owner of collateral its goal is usually to remove it from its balance sheet by selling it at the best possible value and in the shortest timeframe available. What needs to be considered is that some assets may present values that quickly vary over time, and moreover they may require significant maintenance cost, and

Dimension	Description	Example
Actual market value	Each asset has its own marketability depending on how standard it is, current conditions, capability to meet actual technical standards, obsolescence status, design, technology	*Construction equipment easier to sell than a photovoltaic plant*
Transfer Costs	Some assets (e.g. production equipment) are difficult to transfer and the re-sale embeds transportation costs that can be relevant Some equipments need to be disassembled from the plan, transferred and then reassembled if not also revamped	*Industrial robot much easier to transfer than a fundry heavy equipment*
Amount of potential buyers	Some assets might belong to a niche market with few potential buyers E.g. industry specific equipment, some types of commercial vehicles, …	*Mechanical press much easier to sell than a tube end forming machine*
Geographical location of potential buyers	Some assets might not have a market in their home country but they could have some potential abroad E.g. some industries have moved towards lower cost Countries	*Machinery specific to textile industry*
Status of the company	Legal status of a company might prevent from a quick return of the asset E.g. company in bankruptcy vs company in business continuity	*Physical repossessing of an asset from a baknrupt company might take months*

Fig. 7.6 Dimensions to consider for the evaluation of collateral. *Source* Internal analysis

hence they may face different "decay curves" due to macro and micro risk, which may be hedged only partially. This consideration leads to the conclusion that besides focusing on selling economically and efficiently, a bank should also try to pick the right timing, which very much depends of the characteristics of the collateral asset. A further level of complexity derives from the fact that within each category of assets very different kinds of goods can co-exist, as shown in Fig. 7.7, with different decay curves for each one.

Considering for example the real estate assets, it is clear that their value decreases at a lower speed compared to other asset types such as mechanical equipment. This flatter decay curve does not however come free of charge, since, in addition to regular property taxes, maintenance expenses must be sustained in order to preserve their asset value. The overall marketability of the assets is then somewhat constrained by the fact that they cannot be geographically moved, and hence it greatly depends on relative phase of the local real estate economy cycle. If a bank

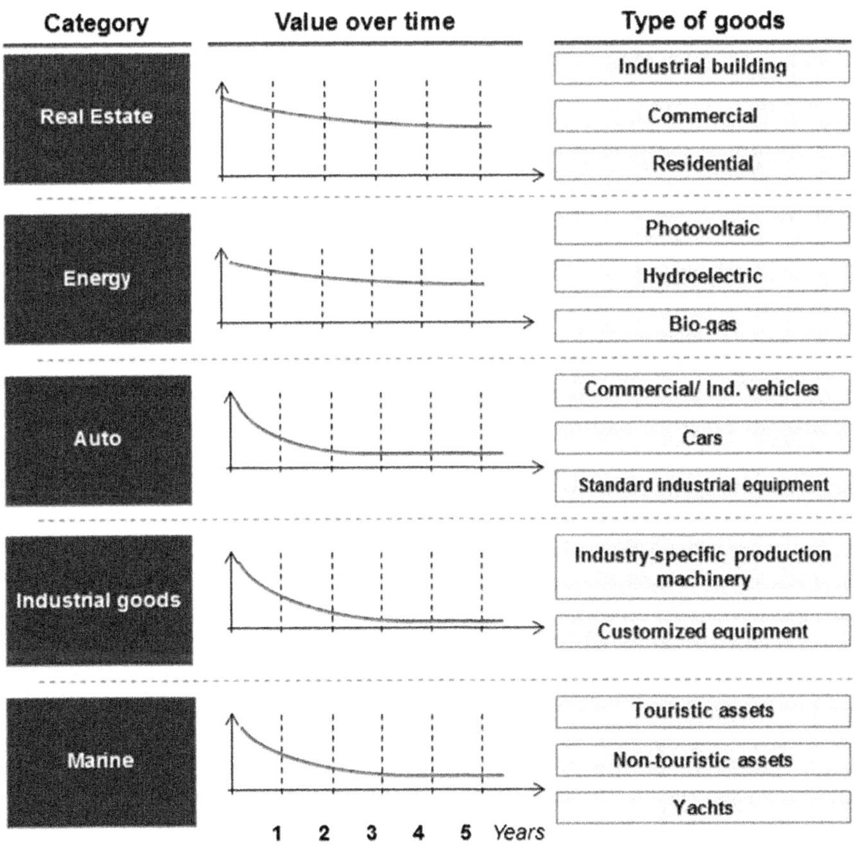

Fig. 7.7 Decay's curves for different kind of collateral. Decay curves for most common assets used as collateral. *Source* Internal analysis

has in place a real estate agency system, such as the one described in the previous chapter, managing or selling collateral of this kind can then become much easier. In any case, there can be different viable strategies. For example, depending on the specificities of the collateral, re-marketing can occur by looking for a new tenant able to replace the old (non performing) one, an investor or a specialized operator in the real estate market or a developer willing to invest and re-qualify the building.

Some of the problems highlighted for real estate assets characterize the renewable energy infrastructural assets as well: in fact, they are also clearly location dependent and require particularly high maintenance costs (for example related to the need of personnel for big plants and technical maintenance for equipment). The value of this class greatly depends on the years the plants is expected to still be employed in production, but generally speaking re-marketing can occur looking for alternative financial investors or for other industrial players in the sector, who may be willing to expand production or significantly transform the assets merging them with their existing production capacity. A different strategy could then consist in treating the assets as if they were "independent companies" and operate a turn around on them. Obviously this solution, while intriguing, requires some knowledge and managerial experience in the field to be carried out.

Car assets can also loose value quickly due to changes in design, technical obsolescence or the introduction of new, competing models. Fortunately, they have relatively low maintenance costs and they are easy to re-market due to the high liquid secondary markets usually in place; they could then be sold in a short span of time before their value moves too much down the decay curve. Commercial vehicles are harder to market, and hence the possibility of selling them through specialized channels, different from those used for commercial cars, should be considered.

The category of industrial goods represents a very heterogeneous asset class, and no univocal comment about its features can be made. For example, while a standard robot can be easily sold and transferred abroad, customized production equipment has a much narrower market and potential buyers can be difficult to find. In any case, this class is characterized by a high level of obsolescence risk, and this fact may force the seller to revamp the assets before re-marketing them.

Finally, maritime assets imply both high maintenance costs (for example harbor fees and personnel for big ships) and a high decay rate, especially in the case of yacht and other commercial assets. Despite these unfavorable aspects, there is the possibility to utilize existing online platforms to market them, although valuations should be carried independently and on an item-by-item basis.

Based on all of the above, it is clear that the assessment and valuation of a portfolio requires a certain level of effort. Nevertheless, it is a necessary and crucial task, because the "as is" value represents the essential starting point for any following re-valuation, which will in turn help in objectively choosing the best workout strategy. As said, it is essential to acknowledge that this value constitutes just part of the valuation: no direct comparison should be made between this measure and what could be obtained in other circumstances, for example under a sale perspective. This is why the following section goes through the relevant factors that need to be taken into account in order to produce a measure that can be used in a relative valuation of best options.

7.6 The "To Be" Value

Once the bank has determined the "as is" value of its portfolio it should move to a "holistic" analysis of the possible actions it can take on it to improve its overall recovery potential. These actions have been broadly discussed in the previous chapters, where we focused on the steps that need to be taken in order to internally manage NPLs. As we have seen, simply managing them and taking restructuring actions on exposures requires a great deal of effort and developing a holistic workout unit is an even more complex task. A bank trying to set up and develop an active management framework has therefore to carefully evaluate the upside potential and build a profit and loss forecast for its recovery activity. Assuming that the timeline of recovery has been defined, this section now focuses on the costs, both explicit and implicit, that such activity entails. In fact, a bank needs to make sure that it does not overlook some components that can have a significant impact on the choice of the best recovery strategy, and specifically on whether the optimal one consists of holding for progress work out or selling for an immediate exit the asset. In order to address these options, there are then three specific issues that need to be considered and analyzed.

The first relates to explicit costs. While the fact that they must be accounted for in the valuation may seem obvious, it is important to properly recognize them, possibly distinguishing between those that are just related to a basic management of the exposure, and are hence inevitable, and those which stem from more extensive actions on the credit itself. Management and recovery costs have to be considered, be them internal, for example administrative and legal expenses, or external, for example those related to credit collectors, fees paid to servicers and for collateral maintenance.

The second element that needs to be accounted for is the recovery speed. It is clear that a perspective valuation of the expected cash-flows cannot disregard the timing at which these will be achieved. In this sense, there may be situations where, even if the internal system is well developed and guarantees higher recovery rates than the external ones, it may be convenient to look at alternative solutions simply because the process takes to long. No valuation can ignore the fact that time has indeed a value, and hence any potential recovery proceed needs to be properly discounted. Recovery speed has a second significant impact on value: in fact, a more efficient process should reduce the time management has to spend on each loan, freeing resources to either increase the volume managed or reduce the aforementioned explicit costs.

Finally, an integrated valuation should take into consideration operating and reputational risks as well. These risks can be of very different kinds, depending on the nature of the exposure and can become very relevant under some circumstances, as in the case of leased goods. In this case in fact, the bank is the direct owner of the asset and therefore it could be held responsible for all or most of the potential liabilities arising from its deterioration or misuse. Just as an example, if bank has leased a dangerous manufacturing factory, it may be forced to either spend significant resources to monitor it, or incur in the risk of massive damage being caused because of lax supervision.

As a last point, the valuation should consider that the management of NPLs, no matter how it is carried out, requires attention and absorbs the time and effort the bank's management. This is true at any level, but even more so when the extent of NPLs becomes such as to pose a threat for the stability of the bank. In this case, besides requiring commitment from parties directly involved in the recovery process, handling NPLs may become a problem of the top management as well. This should always be considered when carrying out a comprehensive valuation, which is then to be compared with what can be achieved through different and multiple options.

7.7 The Overall Assessment of the Strategy

The valuation approach described in the previous paragraph is aimed at identifying the fair value of a certain NPL portfolio (see Fig. 7.8). In the case of NPLs, the assessment of the fair value is particularly critical because it may differ greatly from the book value that was originally recorded by the bank when the loan was issued. In fact, when calculating the fair value of a NPL portfolio we make some basic assumptions: the asset is evaluated at an "average market price" over the cycle, there is no major information asymmetry between the acquirer and the seller, and they have equal bargaining power. These assumptions allow us to calculate a fair value as a price that should be rightfully given to an asset exchanged in a fair transaction. However, the fair value of an asset is not guaranteed to be equal to the market value of the same—actually, because of the very same basic assumptions that were used for its calculation it should differ in some way. The market value at any point in time can then be higher or lower than the fair value or be really close to it: this is because it is the current price at which an asset is sold or bought in the market. The market value strictly depends on the economic cycle and has to be monitored because of its cash flow implications in case of sale. Lastly, we consider the liquidation value. This is the price at which the asset can realistically be sold in the market within a very short time span—sometimes in a fire sale stress scenario; therefore at a value that is usually significantly lower than the market average. Therefore, the liquidation value can also be calculated applying a relevant haircut to the fair value, since we are assuming that a "fire sale" is possible only when selling the asset at a very discounted and attractive market price.

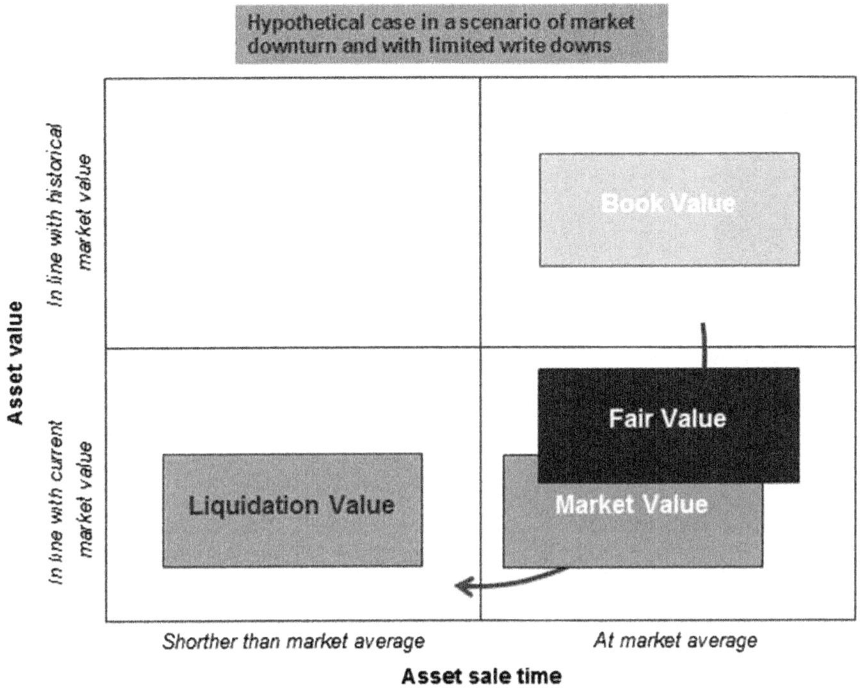

Fig. 7.8 Fair, market and liquidation value for an NPL. Example on different value computations for the same asset. *Source* Internal analysis

A correct assessment of the fair, market and liquidation values for the NPLs portfolio that the bank is evaluating is pretty critical because those prices have the function of influencing the choice on how to manage it for their optimal work out and recovery. In fact, the definition of the best recovery strategy relies mainly on the calculation of the net present value of the portfolio (see Fig. 7.9). In order to get this NPV, the expected cash flows have to be estimated, considering both the recovery of some credit positions and the management or disposal of the underlying collateral. From the total value of the cash flows it must then be subtracted the direct and indirect expenses that the party managing the portfolio will likely incur during the recovery process. Examples of direct expenses are the lawyers' fees and the court expenses for a judicial approach. Indirect costs are instead such things as the employees dedicated to each NPL file, the allocated share of the office expenses or of any other general costs. The net value found must then be discounted at a rate that reflects distressed credit risk, expected property market volatility, target returns and time to recovery. The Net Present Value of the NPL portfolio that has been calculated in this way (basically, the theoretical "to be" or exit value connected to such recovery strategy) needs then to be compared with the fair value and with the market value. We will assume for the sake of simplicity that the fair value is always higher than the market value—although no such universal rule exists and there

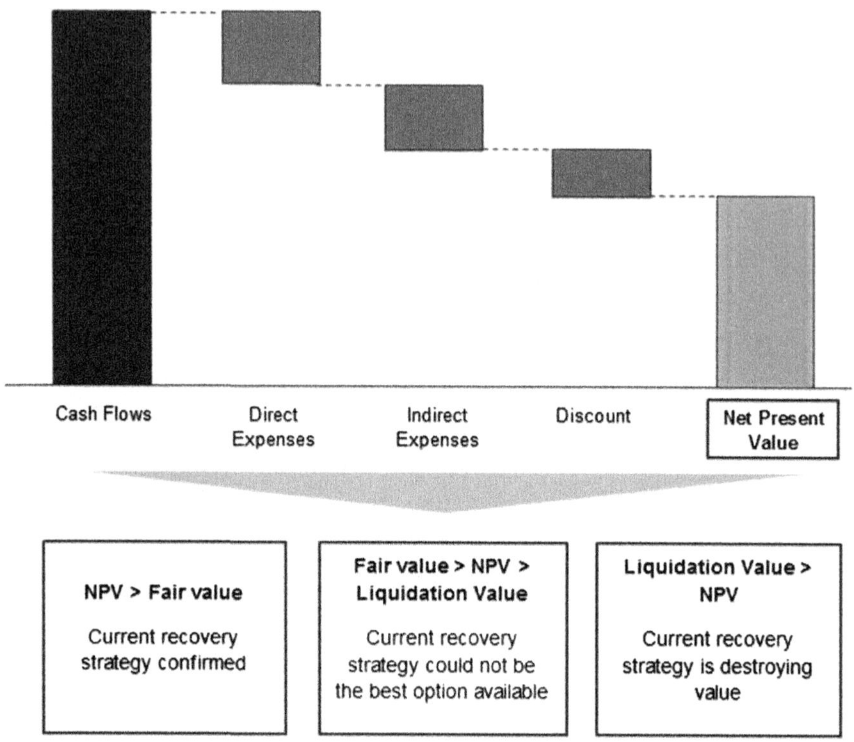

Fig. 7.9 Net present value analysis for an NPL. NPV calculation. *Source* internal analysis

could be extraordinary market conditions proving exactly the opposite (e.g. in a real estate market marked by excess demand).

Once determined the NPV of the portfolio coming from the prospected work out strategy three scenarios can happen. In case the NPV is higher than the fair value of the portfolio, the selected recovery strategy is confirmed: the workout strategy is most probably going to create positive value for the bank, and therefore its internal management is prioritized (unless such a recovery strategy is better pursued with the help and direct drive of a third counterpart). Whenever the NPV value is in between the fair value and the market or liquidation value, the recovery strategy chosen could be not the best one for the bank (it partly closes the gap between the market value and the fair one, but not completely). In such a situation, the bank should consider analysing alternative recovery strategies, or just evaluate the outright disposal (sale) of the NPL portfolio to a third party. When the NPV that the recovery strategy yields is even lower than the market value, the bank would then be clearly better off by selling the loans. The recovery strategy would destroy value—as counterintuitive as it can appear, such cases are frequently popping up, when the extra recovery coming from a given active recovery strategy are not even making up the extra costs incurred to execute such a course of action. In this case, before proceeding with the complete liquidation of the portfolio, a number of alternative options have to be evaluated to minimize the losses.

A further step in the active management of the portfolio would consider some kind of sensitivity analysis that would be required to define alternative options to an internal recovery strategy (see Fig. 7.10). The new options to be considered should be designed for optimizing the recovery value, reducing the time to collection and increasing the volumes collected. A recovery strategy sensitivity model would allow to calculate the return for different approaches to collection that are usually defined according to two main dimensions: the typology of the approach pursued (direct sale, the pursuing of non-judicial or judicial approaches) and the related time needed for the execution, also considering the number of NPL dossiers that are defined within the scope of the work out. As an outcome of the sensitivity analysis related to the above mentioned dimensions, it is possible to find the best approach (internal or external) that will be in charge of the recovery. The sensitivity analysis on different approaches and scenarios will therefore allow to choose the recovery strategy that maximizes the NPV for the bank. Moreover, by setting a "Target Recovery Value", it is possible to set objective hurdle rates on which to measure the performance and value added brought by third parties that could be mandated for the full collection of the portfolio or for just part of it. The last step to be implemented is then a comparison between the internal and external recovery strategies

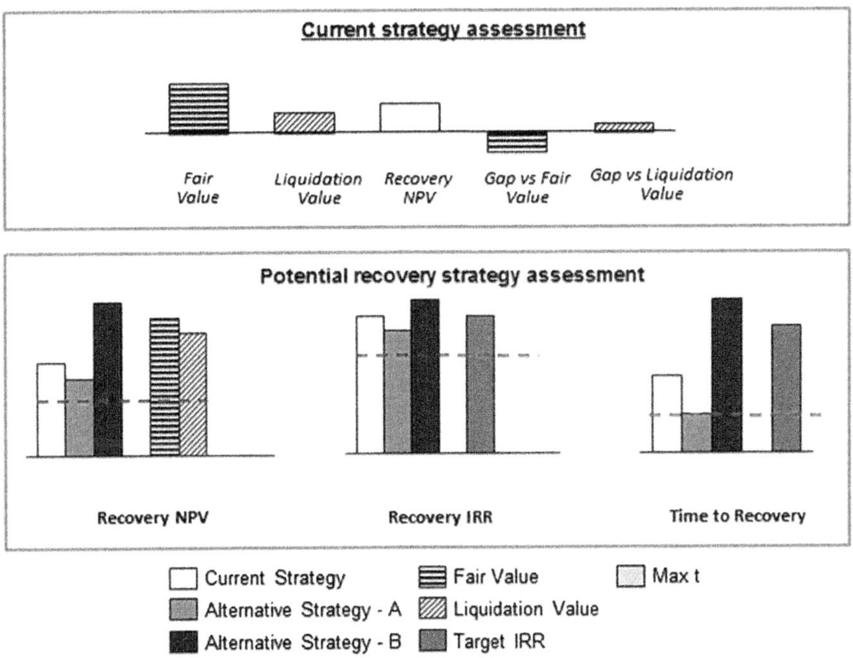

Fig. 7.10 Assesment of different recovery strategies. Comparison between current and potential recovery strategy. *Source* Internal analysis

that have been identified with the sensitivity analysis. The performance gap, that represents the potential improvement in the current recovery strategies being pursued through external credit workouts, will then be cross checked via a full comparison of a number of other KPIs calculated in the model. Each of these KPIs will also be used for comparing the current workout performance with both objective market targets and with what has been achieved by peers.

7.8 Defining the Best Set of Actions

In this chapter we have provided several definitions of "value" for a NPL, and suggested different approaches to determine this. The fact that value cannot be determined in a unique way should neither be considered as confusing, nor surprising. In fact, as a general rule valuation is inevitably a process that requires a certain degree of subjectivity and more importantly so for NPLs, as—similarly to any other asset—they are not worth the same for all parties, and hence multiple valuations exist. For this reason, a bank should evaluate portfolios under different perspectives, in order to identify the best option leading to the highest recovery value and the connected optimal workout strategy (see Fig. 7.11). The result will also show whether the bank has a distinctive set of skills and capabilities that make it suited for managing NPLs internally. If it has no advantage in terms of market power, management skills or efficiency, the best solution may be to resort to external servicers or simply to liquidate the asset on the market, even if this may imply selling them at a significant discount vis a vis the book value. The outcome

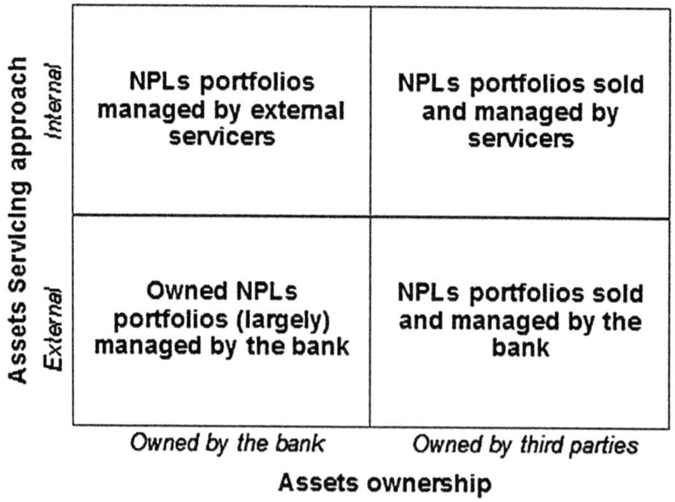

Fig. 7.11 Multiple options for ownership and servicing. Options for NPL ownership and management. *Source* Internal analysis

can lead to very different settings, with NPLs having a different level of importance in each of them. Figure 7.11 illustrates how it is possible to cathegorize them on the basis of asset ownership and asset servicing approach.

The top left box represents the area of credit workout as a "captive" affair: the bank maintains the ownership of the loans and it manages most of them internally. This requires having an effective and holistic workout unit in place, where the increased complexity associated with its development should be more than compensated by greater recovery rates. In fact, if a bank is positioned in this area it means that the estimated "to be" value, which takes into account all the explicit and implicit costs that need to be sustained, is higher than what could be achieved by simpler solutions. The opposite box on the same side of the matrix, is instead characterized by the portion of loans that, even if still owned by the bank, are not managed internally, either because they are not sufficiently large to justify internal management or because outsourcing is a more efficient and effective alternative anyway. In this case, the value of the loan would be given by the expected recovery that can be achieved by the servicer, obviously netted of the fees that will need to be paid to it.

In the bottom-right box, we find credit work out companies that operate just as credit collection servicers: they do not own the loans and are hence not entitled to the recovery flow, but they profit from a "success fee" that they get from the party which owns the asset. Credit work out units could be, by the way, partially owned by banks that may have chosen to sell a relevant a portion of their NPLs to reduce their risk (removing them from their book), but that at the same time have pursued the development of their internal work out units via alliances and Joint Ventures and not only to manage the remaining portion of their loans, but also to offer their collection services to other third parties for a fee. Eventually, they could also keep acting as servicers for the external parties to which the bank may eventually end up selling its NPLs: in fact, they would have already all the data required and they would receive fees, while at the same time increasing the total volume of loans managed, with likely costs savings thanks to the economies of scale achieved. Finally, the top right area is constituted by loans sold and managed by third parties. In this case the bank estimates that the value that can be obtained on the market is higher than what could be achieved through other options. This can be due to the fact that the NPLs are being overvalued by the buyers, or more likely that their recovery approaches are much more efficient and effective, thus allowing to both the seller and the buyer to be better off—with a share of the extra value to be negotiated.

Whatever the final organizational solution, dedicating attention to the valuation process is by no means a waste of time and it plays in multiple critical way a major role in crafting and executing the chosen recovery strategy. In fact information asymmetries make it hard to assess the true value of each component, and hence without a careful analysis a bank risks losing great part of the potential recovery, either because it sells at prices way below fair value or because it embarks in lengthy and resource consuming recovery processes that are not justified by economic fundamentals. Unfortunately there exists no magic recipe to overcome the problem, but some actions illustrated in this chapter, such as building a database in which all relevant information is stored and regularly verified and updated and then developing a sophisticated and dynamic dashboard to plan and control the active management of NPLs and of their collaterals, are certainly a good starting point.

Chapter 8
The WHAM of a Troubled Corporate Loans Portfolio

Abstract Credit work out is mostly focused on non performing loans. However, particularly when the collateral is mostly related to the going concern of the debtor company, the best recovery strategy should be aimed at keeping the counterpart from becoming not performing—almost at all costs. The proactive management of sub performing loans to corporates stands therefore as an interesting area to be consider for the development and augmentation of the services offered by any "alpha playing" credit work out. The best management of troubled corporates involves usually some kind of "hard" restructuring, where new management, fresh capital, some change in governance and the help of professional turn around advisors can ensure a more likely and speedy recovery of the company and of the loans attached to it. Again, a holistic and active restructuring is the best option to consider as the company has a number of tangible and intangible values to preserve.

Keywords Corporate restructuring · Credit workout · Sub performing loans · Holistic turnaround

8.1 Corporate Restructuring and Credit Work Out

So far our discussion, besides a few exceptions, has been mostly focused on how to handle NPLs: the analysis has been centered on what to do once the chances of repayment from a debtor get close to zero and the only way to recover part of the value is through the implementation of an effective credit workout strategy—often focused on the repossession and the following sale of the collateral. An active credit workout strategy for NPLs that focuses on the repossession and sale of the collateral can work well for some sorts of credits, and particularly those which are highly collateralized and whose residual value can hence be recovered through a proper management of the guarantees, often a real estate asset, as in the case of residential loans. While in these situations the workout unit can effectively handle the credit even after it has become non performing, recovery on defaulted loans is much more

C. Scardovi, *Holistic Active Management of Non-Performing Loans*,
DOI 10.1007/978-3-319-25363-3_8

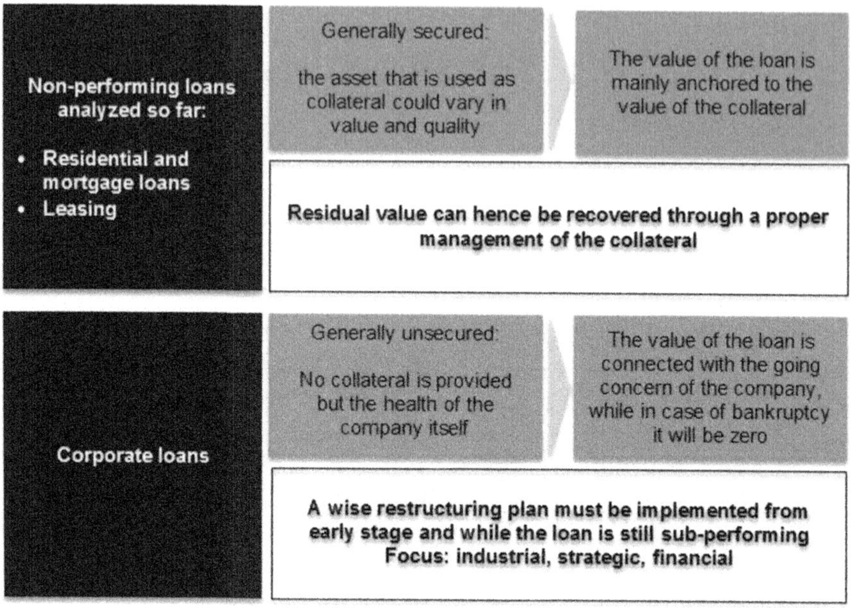

Fig. 8.1 Summary of NPLs potential nature and structure

difficult in the case of credits to corporates which are not properly backed by tangible assets—e.g. its recovery value ends up being strongly correlated with the going concern of the company, or at least most part of it (see Fig. 8.1). When the company stops having a "going concern" and it gets close to liquidation, the residual value of a corporate loan can in fact only come from either what can be recovered through some liquidation procedures or what can be obtained by selling out single parts of the bankrupt firm. It follows that, unless proper actions are taken to safeguard the company since the earliest signs of trouble, a strategy just focused on the value recoverable from the collateral will lead to poor results, as the firm would have lost all the goodwill (as client portfolios, know-how, team of talents and so on) it built during its life.

Following this line of reasoning, it is clear that a bank should set up proactive procedures aimed at preserving the value of its credits towards corporations, by way of constant monitoring and proactive management of the situations that are most likely to get in some form of distress. On one side, the bank must act to ensure that the company chances of continuing its operations are maximized: this means taking on holistic view to support the counterpart and make sure to reduce its probability of default. On the other side, it can act on the loss given default of its exposure: while for some companies the problems may be so severe that bankruptcy is inevitable, the value that can be obtained in the phase of liquidation can be increased by putting in place safeguard mechanisms much earlier on. This can be done if the management of the company will develop in advance an orderly plan that can ensure that most of the intangible value of the company (in terms of network of clients, brand name, commercial portfolio of contracts, etc.) does not get disrupted or entirely lost following its bankruptcy. Such contingency plan should not be limited to companies with clearly distressed situations, but cover as well firms which appear to be (still) solid, but with uncertain future perspectives: in fact, as the financial crisis has highlighted, value can disappear in the span of a few days. As in the case of Lehman Brothers: following the bankruptcy, most of its remaining value was lost because of the loss of talents' teams, clients' relationships and commercial contracts, not to mention the suboptimal unwinding of still valuable financial portfolios.

Even an apparently strong and well matured goodwill can entirely and quickly be lost unless safeguard procedures are established, with the help of specialised restructuring and liquidating advisors. Given the strong interconnectedness between the value of a company and that of its debts towards banks, we see therefore a strong rationale for introducing a chapter on corporate restructuring in a book on NPLs. In this chapter we first analyze the possible options available to a bank in order to handle its sub performing corporate loans proactively and holistically. And we will also discuss briefly the most prominent approaches to corporate restructuring.

8.2 Sub Performing Corporate Loans: The Ways Out

The strategies a bank can pursue when facing a significant surge in sub performing corporate loans are multiple, but they can essentially be broken down in two macro categories: sell (at a discount) or actively manage (within the limits of what allowed by the specific lending situation and the relevant bankruptcy Law) the remaining exposure. The distinction is somewhat similar to what we have already discussed for non performing loans in general: a bank can either choose to sell outright its exposure, removing the bad position from its balance sheet but foregoing part of the possible recovery value (the discount incorporated in the sale price), or undertake extensive pre workout actions in order to be an active party—albeit indirect, and with all the constraints introduced by the relevant Law—in the restructuring and turn around plan of the company, sometimes even assuming an equity position in it as a result of the debt to equity partial or full conversion.

When analyzing the sale perspective, it can be noticed that in the case of corporate loans there exists a multitude of specialized players (private equity and vulture funds) interested in buying risky loans from banks when they are still sub performing. This is especially true now, as this kind business has been growing after the global financial crisis that started in 2008. On one side, low interest rates have guaranteed an increased availability of cheap financing, and thus and increased demand from investors looking for higher yields. On the other, given the huge amount of sub performing loans that come out of the crisis, funds have a massive pool of raw material on which they can work. A bank wanting to actively address its exposure towards a distressed company can pursue therefore two alternative options. The first relies in trying to convert its debt into equity in order to sell its stake to a private equity fund (or lead, as the main shareholder, the restructuring and turn around of the corporate). The second could instead involve selling the exposure directly to debt funds which then pursue (usually in more aggressive terms) a "debt-to-own" strategy (e.g. seeking to convert the debt into equity, and building parallel equity stakes so to take the control of the company). In fact, these investors usually aim at holding a relevant portion (over 50 %) of the overall loans towards a company, so that by becoming the major creditor they have the power to promote and push a more aggressive and timely restructuring of the company, to keep it viable and thus allowing a greater performance on their investment. While these second option is certainly an easier strategy for a bank that wants to remove a sub performing credit from its balance sheet, it does not usually maximize the value that can be recovered (at least from the bank's perspective, as the private equity/vulture funds will tend to buy at huge discount vis a vis the nominal value of the loan). Private equity funds usually target a 12–18 % IRR for their investment on such loans, which means that the bank will be able to liquidate its stake only at a very high discount. As an "easy" way out to get rid of troubled loans, selling to financial sponsors is indeed not a cheap solution!

The alternative strategy that a bank could consider would involve the proactive handling of the credit portfolio, in order to avoid its immediate sale in order to maximize its value in the medium—long term. The problem for most banks is that they do not hold a sufficiently large credit stake for them to be able to take any effective action that could have some impact on the company. In fact, when the total debt financing of a company is widely dispersed and fragmented, no creditor alone has the power to exercise relevant control over the company and to force on it the restructuring plan that it would need in order to survive (something the current shareholders and management, for a number of different reasons, may be unwilling to consider). This is why banks need to act together in order to obtain an overall greater negotiating power with the company and more effectively "moral suade" its current shareholders and management to take action. In fact, as long as the company does not default on its obligations and the creditors do not convert their stake into equity, action can only take the form of moral suasion; but even with these limitations pressure from creditors to restructure and implement corrective actions can prove very valuable.

A possible problem for banks trying to pursue this strategy on their own is that, since agreement among many counterparties can be very cumbersome and take very long, action may not be as prompt as it would be needed and coordination costs may become a relevant issue. Moreover, banks may not possess the skills that are necessary to develop a strategy that takes into account an industrial perspective besides a more financial one. This is why an increasingly appealing strategy is to resort to third party managed active restructuring funds. These are set ups, or "platforms", that have the capabilities and the scale required for effectively handling a large number of sub performing loans. These funds could also allow to the bank the derecognition of the troubled assets, lightening its balance sheet and freeing

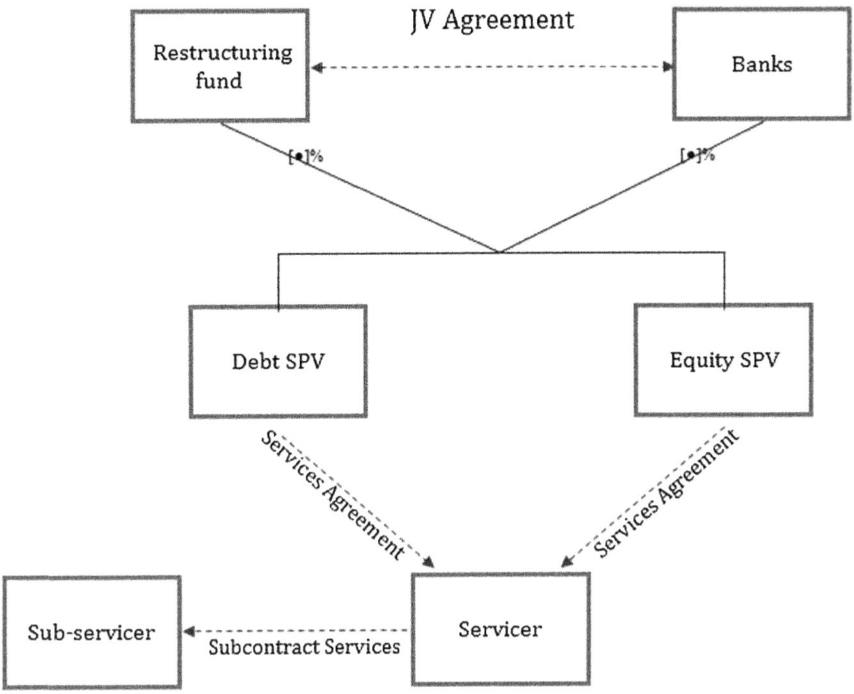

Fig. 8.2 A potential structure for a "platform" approach. JV structure. *Source* Internal analysis

regulatory capital. There are different possible legal structures for them. A possible solution would be to create a joint venture, directly or indirectly participated by the restructurer (usually a professional advisor), by the private equity ready to inject new money to finance the restructuring and the potentially needed capital raise and by the banks. The fund would then acquire and refinance sub performing credits in order to manage them (see Fig. 8.2).

One suggested structure for such actively managed funds would for example consider two different SPVs (Special Purpose Vehicle): a debt SPV, which would be a securitization vehicle with different compartments holding the loans transferred from the various participating banks, and an equity SPV, which would hold equity or quasi equity instruments that cannot be held by the debt SPV. This approach guarantees that each asset transferred by the banks will automatically represent a separate compartment, and hence creditors will only be able to satisfy their claims on the assets or the proceeds related to their specific compartment. Moreover, asset segregation keeps investors secured from potential insolvencies of other assets or of the JV itself. These SPVs could then have their credits managed by external providers (e.g. restructuring companies) through services/consulting agreements that will be assigned based on the best track record and experience.

When compared with the direct sale approach, it is clear that this management strategy allows banks to extract more value from their positions: in fact, by acting as catalysts of the recovery processes rather than being passive and simply selling out their credits, they are able to have more contractual power towards the company and can hence participate in the upside from value creation.

Such value comes from the proactive management of the credits and of the company itself, aimed at maximizing the return on investment and the amount recovered. This involves identifying and executing, whenever possible and appropriate, operational, commercial and financial restructuring initiatives. As already said, as long as the debtor respects the covenants of its credits, restructurers cannot take direct action. Nevertheless, given the higher contractual power gathered together by all the parties involved, even moral suasion can prove to be a very effective measure at this stage. The next section provides some insight on the possible actions, both industrial and financial, that are typically carried out in order to make a distressed company viable again trough its restructuring.

8.3 Corporate Restructuring: An Overview

There are many reasons that can bring a company to a situation of financial distress and action can take place at different levels. In order to ensure an effective restructuring, realizing that a company must not only develop a good strategy and ensure proper execution, but also choosing the right timing for this is key. In fact, unless actions are taken at an early stage of distress, it may become increasingly difficult to obtain the desired results, and this is why it is necessary to be able to spot early signals that may predict distress in order to act promptly and maximize the restructuring plan's effects. While identifying some kind of problems, whose visibility is very high, is relatively easy, the task may become harder when dealing with more eradicated issues. Given the importance of timely recognition of situation of financial distress, we provide a brief overview of the main reasons that may erode a company's performance and of the indicators that should be considered in order to identify the underlying problems. We will then move to analyzing the actions that can be implemented in order to restructure a company.

8.3.1 Company Crisis: Reasons and Indicators

A company's distress may manifest in different forms, but the final stage, the one immediately preceding its failure, is usually taking place in the form of a liquidity crisis: the company cannot face its obligations and it is hence exposed to the risk of imminent bankruptcy. Liquidity crisis can be triggered by several factors both endogenous and exogenous. For example, a company with an already precarious liquidity structure (excessive amount of receivables or unsecured credits and low financial reserves) may face an unexpected external event, for example the increase of interest rates or the cancellation of part of its bank loans, which may push it into some kind of cash shortage. Whatever the trigger event, liquidity crisis can be easily anticipated by looking at simple financial indicators and trends of key balance sheet values, such as the amount of contingent liabilities, the level of unresolved near term debt maturities, the amount of outstanding account payables and the aging of account receivables: a deterioration in any of these would act as a clear alarm for distress.

Despite the fact that, thanks to the high visibility of the symptoms behind them, the identification of liquidity crisis is easy, dealing with them is very difficult: even if the problems are identified early on, the company is already in a phase of deep distress and close to bankruptcy, so that the scope for action for a restructurer is very limited. Its focus can indeed be at best on taking short term actions aimed at buying time for the company. This is why limiting action to this last stage is not sufficient, and a restructurer should be able to identify earlier stages signals and at a different level, as before incurring in liquidity problems, companies usually face other kinds of distress. These are harder to identify, because the underlying symptoms are much less visible, but action at this stage could ensure a much greater efficacy and be open to the broadest set of alternatives.

For example, a company may face a profit crisis, through which lower and lower after tax earnings are achieved, and could eventually turn into losses, progressively eroding its capital base. The worsening of the bank's profitability can then be deduced by looking at the EBITDA trend over time: a shrinking margin may be due to a decrease in revenues, an insufficient cost to income efficiency or to a combination of both of these aspects. A high management turnover or unplanned reductions in workforce can also contribute to instability. External factors, such as market saturation, volatility in the exchange rate for companies deriving a significant amount of revenues abroad or political instability in the Countries of production can also play a relevant role. While some of these events are clearly unpredictable, it is essential to look both at features that are specific to the company, such as whether it has an outdated product portfolio and, if so, how active is the product development pipeline, but also to its macro characteristics, such as the regulatory environment and the overall industry outlook, in order to assess the extent of distress. Given this approach, it may be now clearer why—when discussing the best options for creating a database for loans—we stressed so much the relevance of gathering information of industrial nature and of establishing a system of early warning signals. In fact, establishing trigger values for parameters that can signal the approaching of a profit crisis, and taking actions if the predetermined levels are overcome, is a good way to maximize the chances of identifying just in time this kind of distress.

Finally, it is also possible to intervene with a restructuring plan on companies experiencing a strategic crisis. These are firms who lack the factors that can guarantee long term success, although there are still fine in terms of short term performance. Their long term viability at risk could be due to endogenous factors, such as the fact that they operate in an industry which is entering in a deep and prolonged recession or for which there has been a significant breakthrough which will completely change consumers' demand. Realizing that the whole business is not viable in the longer term may be difficult. Nevertheless, intervention on companies that have accounting issues, are stifled by red tape or corruption or do not follow a clear strategy or are under investing on new products, can stop them from pursuing no return roads and refocus on a more attractive business.

Depending on the level on which it acts, the focus of the restructurer may shift from ensuring the mere survival of the company, to giving it a stable and sustainable profit base to even redefining its whole business model. The next section explores the options that can be implemented.

8.3.2 Early Actions: Institutionalizing Cash Management

After having understood the reasons behind the crisis of the company, it is important to implement targeted actions in order to deal with it since an early stage. The first thing that has to be taken into control is the cash management of the company: a distressed firm could easily burn lot of cash simply by carrying out its normal day to day operations (think for example of a highly positive net working capital that absorbs cash even when the company is just implementing the most basic and daily activities). Therefore, optimizing the cash management of the company becomes critical in order to stop value destruction and turn it into value preservation or possibly value creation.

The best way to approach the task is creating a dedicated and specialized unit that is in charge of institutionalizing cash management. The aim of such unit is to avoid any liquidity crisis in the short term while the cash management is reorganized and executed. The job is particularly delicate because a lot of dimensions and of company's aspects have to be taken in consideration. For example, there are some levers, such as products pricing, sales commissions or incentives that should be managed carefully, because the risk is to improve the company's cash situation in the very short term, while destroying real value (think for example of the effect on sales if the price is increased without any plausible reason). Regulatory constraints must be considered as well, in order to come out with a management plan that is truly implementable and sustainable for the long term. After having identified what are the constraints that the new cash management plan should consider, it is necessary to analyze what are the cash generation possibilities that should be actively exploited to optimize the firm's cash reserves for immediate and short term use.

We can identify four main dimensions through which it is possible to sort out ways to maximize cash flows in the short run (see Fig. 8.3). First of all, we should look at new sources of short term funding that would support the cash flows in a first phase. This could be achieved through access to bank accounts or possibly by issuing new equity (notice that the latter is not feasible in many countries, where the equity issuing process is very long and cumbersome). But the most important and effective dimension on which to act is usually the relationship with commercial suppliers and clients. The renegotiation of cash flow terms with suppliers is

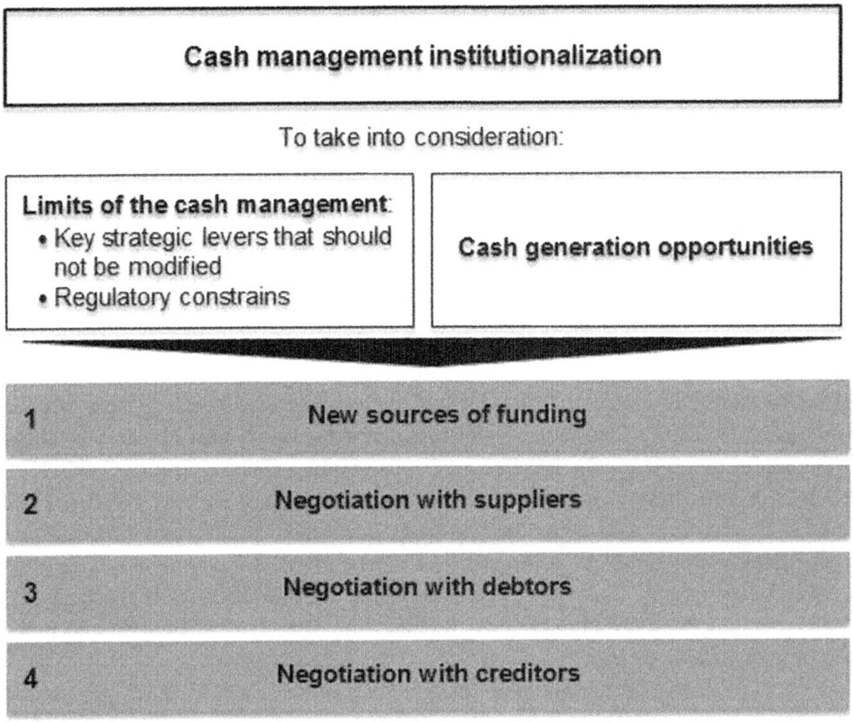

Fig. 8.3 A general framework for optimal cash management. Cash management process. *Source* Own experience

finalized at obtaining better conditions that would help the company refinance its operations in the short run. As it can be imagined, a distressed company does not have a strong negotiating power: the hypothesis of a future bankruptcy could by itself rise the cost of credit or even lead some suppliers to chose to terminate or suspend the commercial relationship with the company. Therefore it is important to carefully analyze the standing relationship with suppliers, to understand which one are key for the company, to determine the value of the relationship with such suppliers (in terms of what effect it has in the company's revenues, costs and income), to explore possible alternatives and to identify what kind of negotiating strategy could be ideally pursued. Negotiation with the company's commercial clients must be carried on as well in parallel. The plan must aim at reducing the time needed to recover the credits with the company's counterparts and sustain faster payments. The objective of such negotiation is however to avoid that such short term repayments drain up the client's financing capacity, therefore increasing the credit risk on such outstanding positions.

8.3.3 Determining the Value of Options for Shareholders

A further step to take is assessing what are the value creating options available for the stakeholders. It is important to identify what are the available opportunities for the company to improve and make sure it exploits them. We can find value creation opportunities in three directions mainly.

First of all, the analysis of the value creation chain could allow highlighting what are the factors through which the company creates value on an "as is" basis. On this basis, the processes that are value driven should be identified and made more efficient for the maximization of their outcome. A second dimension to be addressed is external growth strategies: it must be determined if the company can solve part of its problem by seeking external acquisitions, partnerships or divestitures. For example, the restructuring could include the divestiture of some of the firm's asset in order to refocus on the core business or on the sectors that allow bigger margins, higher cash balances and profitability. This concept is addressed also by the third dimension that could involve a complete strategy overhaul and business redefinition, refocusing the company on its core competencies or investing to establishing new ones. After the business perspectives of the company have been identified, it is in any case necessary to evaluate them and assess if the expected value creation targets are high enough to justify the restructuring process and make the company viable again.

Such analysis can be implemented using standard valuation methods adjusted in order to consider the effects of the distressed situation. To that extent, to complete the valuation, a scenario analysis is usually performed, in order to assess what could be the possible directions that the firm would get with or without restructuring. Important elements to take into consideration while performing the analysis are the financial value of the firm, the actual risk that the restructuring process carries, the chances of corporate survival as well as the interests that stakeholders have in the company.

The valuation of the company as it is and of the claims towards it has to be compared to the one that it would possibly have when properly restructured. This implies confronting the enterprise value with and without restructuring. If the value of the claims on the firm is covered only when the restructured enterprise value is considered, then it is clear that a restructuring process should be enough to avoid bankruptcy and be considered instead of an accelerated liquidation of the company.

As part of the valuation process, the optimal capital structure has also to be identified. When determining the optimal debt capacity, we need to consider the trade off between the tax shield benefit and the cost in terms of financial distress of additional debt and the forgone financial flexibility. This analysis comprises the identification of the target debt rating, its comparison with industry benchmarks, and the identification of the leverage that minimizes the cost of capital.

8.3.4 Assessing Restructuring Options

Restructuring can be carried out in different fashions according to the several instruments and options made available by the relevant Law of any Country. While these differ among nations, and hence there exists no clear cut separation that can be univocally applied all over the world, a general distinction can be set between pre-insolvency remedies and post-insolvency procedures (see Fig. 8.4).

In the first category one may include different kind of options, but all of them have to be consensual—as there is no formal bankruptcy procedure yet, parties involved cannot be forced to implement actions against their will: actions need therefore to be debtor driven. Options in this category can range from actions that are entirely executed out of court, as in the case of turnaround plans, to solutions already closer to a proper insolvency procedure. In the first case, since the majority of the creditors have to agree on a restructuring plan, reaching consensus may be more difficult, but if the plan is implemented in this way, this guarantees the highest level of confidentiality, as the whole procedure is conducted privately. A second option can be a debt restructuring agreement: debt can be exchanged through a tender offer for either cash at a discount or a combination of securities, such as a combination of equity and debt, where the maturity and interest on the new debt are revised with respect to the previous conditions. Finally, the already mentioned pre-insolvency composition constitutes an evolution of the private workout procedure, which in addition aims at capturing the possible benefits deriving from in-court proceedings.

When a company approaches default or falls into default, the only option is resorting to insolvency procedures. These could either provide protection to the company in order to maximize its chances to continue its operation in some way, for example by including debtor in possession financing under some jurisdictions and automatic stay options, or limit its actions to liquidation in the case of definitive bankruptcy (see Fig. 8.5). The relative convenience of these two different approaches can vary depending on the considerations on several factors. Private

	Pre-insolvency remedies	Insolvency Procedures
Effects on company	• Possibly lower dilution of shareholders' interest • No court-imposed restrictions on business	• Negative reputational impact • High disclosure requirements
Feasibility considerations	Difficulties related with: • Availability of interested investors • Capital structure complexity • Existence of clauses on change of control	• No issues related to tender offer holdouts • Only possible option for companies facing imminent default

Fig. 8.4 Pre-insolvency remedies and post-insolvency procedures. Pre-insolvency and insolvency procedures. *Source* Internal analysis

Turnaround Plan	Debt restructuring agreement	Pre-insolvency composition
✓ Outside court ✓ Higher confidentiality	✓ Redefinition of debt terms ✓ Limited automatic stay	✓ Cram down ✓ Full automatic stay
✗ No cram down ✗ No automatic stay	✗ No cram down ✗ Formal procedure	✗ In court procedure

Fig. 8.5 Potential options: a comparison. Pre-insolvency versus insolvency. *Source* Internal analysis

work outs seem to be preferable to bankruptcy procedures for what concerns shareholders' value after restructuring. In fact, distribution of value in the case of an in-court procedure tends to be focused on preserving the rights of creditors given priority rules, while through a workout procedure shareholders may be able to withstand the current distress of the company and recover a greater part of their investment.

Moreover a workout, when compared to the alternative of entering a formal procedure, is less disruptive for the company: in fact, in this case the courts cannot impose any legal restrictions on the business. Finally, when a private restructuring is carried out, the reputation of the firm is partially eroded, but the public perception and the extent of the confidence in the company is way higher than what would happen in the case of a filing for bankruptcy. Despite these benefits, private work out entails several difficulties from the point of view of execution, and hence in some circumstances it cannot be considered a feasible option. Specifically, in cases when the company has a very complex capital structure or change-of-control provisions that limit the possibility of selling through a private procedure a significant portion of its equity, it may be hard to reach an agreement to operate a private work out. Moreover, the absence of parties interested in implementing a cash tender offer may constitute a significant obstacle. Finally, in some circumstances the company may be so close to default that a private workout is just not feasible.

8.4 The Importance of a Holistic Turnaround Approach

The target of a restructuring plan is not just about the identification of the key areas and of the most critical issues that have to be addressed and fixed, but also about designing an appropriate approach in order to reach value maximization. When talking about corporate restructuring, we have to keep in mind that the first priority relates to value preservation. A holistic turnaround approach advocates then for an active management of the company in distress aimed at stopping value destruction from a very early stage and at introducing operational improvements for the medium long term horizon (see Fig. 8.6). Following a well established approach, restructuring is usually based on the definition of the company's business model, the renegotiation of the capital and funding structure of the company and on the implementation of the actual turn around plan. While this process might seem linear and within an easy reach, it fails in avoiding destroying part of the company's value during the first two phases—as the actual implementation of the industrial and financial recommendations is delayed.

A holistic approach, whose main focus would be on operational improvements, would instead look at starting the implementation since an earlier stage, working in parallel with the business model and capital and funding structuring workstreams. Upfront operational improvements will then allow to better preserve the company's value for the benefit of all the stakeholders, allowing also a full understanding of the company that can support the design of further medium long term actions. The two processes, traditional and holistic are compared in Fig. 8.6.

In a holistic approach, the preservation of the company value becomes the key element that has to be taken into consideration and dealt with. Some actions may be aimed at enhancing the company's EBITDA, through such drivers as the active management of the business portfolio (including disposals and sales of non core

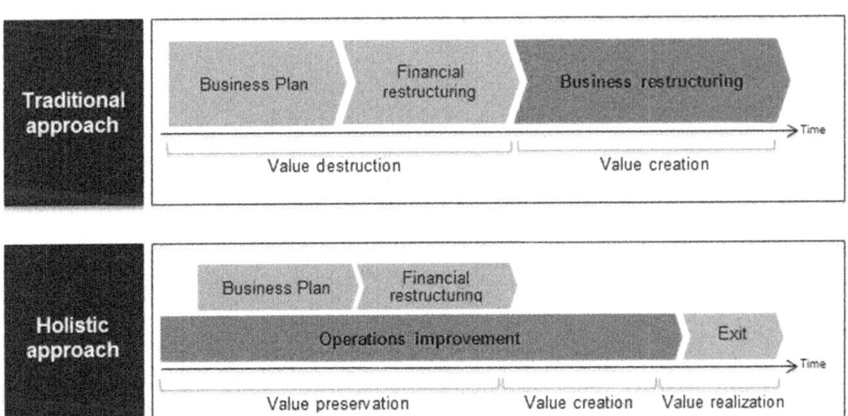

Fig. 8.6 Restructuring approach: traditional versus holistic. Traditional approach to business restructuring versus holistic approach. *Source* Internal analysis

assets), the optimization of the manufacturing footprint, and the operating costs reduction. All these kind of actions are designed to improve the performance in an accelerated way through the identification of inefficiencies, untapped potential and opportunities.

Other actions relate instead to optimal cash management, net working capital reduction and asset monetization and are aimed at preserving and maximizing the available cash and mid term funding.

The holistic approach focuses overall on three main objectives. Firstly, an effective restructuring plan should allow taking effective control of the company: the change has to be implemented with the support of a strong and experienced leadership that allows crisis stabilization in the first place and needs to have all the relevant managerial levers at its disposal. Secondly, a restructuring plan should be able to reach the consensus and support of the main stakeholders. Thirdly, the restructuring plan should aim at fixing the business as a whole and for the long run. This can be achieved by shifting the strategic focus to more feasible targets, by improving the organizational structure and effectiveness and by enhancing the critical processes and their operational efficiency.

Chapter 9
The WHAM of a Real Estate Loans Portfolio

Abstract Banks from all over the world are long on real estate assets—even more so in Europe where banks could arguably be defined as the biggest "real estate companies" in the region, as they lend to real estate developers and to their buyers (not to mention how many real estate assets they own directly). Given such a long position, for an optimal credit work out of NPLs, specific real estate skills and know how are required, and the processes and tools of the "alpha platform" have to be built to ensure the best management of those assets: these could include new initiatives (or "accelerators") as the already introduced "real estate agency" and "real estate owned company". The comprehensive approach to the WHAM of a real estate backed NPLs portfolio is defined and explained, with a specific focus on the underlyings (AREM: active real estate management).

Keywords Real estate · Interconnections · Real estate assets management · Active space management · AREM · Active real estate management

9.1 Banking and the Real Estate Sector—The Interconnections

The multiple and deep interconnectedness between the real estate sector and the banking one have been already discussed when talking about the best set up strategy for an active credit workout unit. In that context, we explored the role that "tools" such as a bank owned real estate agency or a real estate owned company can play in the workout process: indeed we said that they can work as enablers and accelerators, facilitating the active management and value optimization of the collateral. While setting up these enablers constitutes undoubtedly a right step in the path towards becoming an active player in the real estate sector, there are certainly other actions that need to be taken for a bank to become, if not a "real estate player", at least a "real estate" savvy risk manager.

C. Scardovi, *Holistic Active Management of Non-Performing Loans*,
DOI 10.1007/978-3-319-25363-3_9

This second set of actions includes measures that are maybe more innovative and stand as a breakthrough vis a vis what is typically considered to be a classic banking activity. Indeed they are not simply aimed at finding clever ways of acting on the real estate collateral of a borrower in order to preserve its value, but they may even entail the development of new business areas which are revenues producing and therefore adding to the overall value creation capacity of the bank.

When discussing about the workout unit "accelerators", we discussed how the reasons that supported the idea of a bank developing specific knowledge and competencies in the real estate field were related to its ability to properly assess the value of the real estate assets that were used as collateral to its loans. Only by having strong real estate valuation competencies a bank can be able to assess the risks coming from the deterioration in value of the collateral, and consequently prevent such a loss. Moreover, once the borrower has defaulted and the bank became the owner of the collateral, having knowledge in the real estate sector stand as the only way to properly evaluate the asset and choose the best active management option. There are actually many more situations in which a bank may need to deal with real estate assets: the next section analyzes which are the typical real estate related assets we may find in a bank portfolio. We then move to discuss the potential implications for the bank management and the tools that need to address them.

9.2 How Many Real Estate Assets Does a Bank Have in Its Portfolio?

Depending on which kind of definition of real estate asset's "ownership" is considered, the amount of real estate related assets in a bank's portfolio can vary greatly. In any case, regardless of whether a narrower or broader definition is applied, it is clear that real estate plays a major role in the balance sheet of any bank. At a very first level, one must consider that each bank owns a certain number of real estate assets. These include on one side all the assets that are needed for operational reasons, such as branches and administrative offices, and on the other direct investment properties, which may have a sizeable value. Among its owned assets one must also include the repossessed assets that the bank has acquired following the default of its debtors; in the case in which a bank has a REOCO (real estate owned company) in place, the number of assets included in this category could be particularly high, as there would be a specific structure aimed at acquiring properties. Also, a bank is the legal owner of all the assets related to the business of real estate leasing.

At a second level, despite the fact that it is not the owner, a bank has to consider the real estate properties connected with its lending activity. This category includes both assets related to retail mortgages and properties connected with real estate development projects. The latter deserve special attention, since they usually stand as a substantial part of a bank loans portfolio.

These can be concentrated towards different stages of the construction process, starting from brown field and moving to green field and finished properties. Monitoring the project to assess whether it is on track and its chances of completion are high enough to guarantee the full recovery of the credit is essential if a bank wants to avoid having to write-down part of its loan. This implies that a bank has to be able to understand the project under different perspectives: not only it must identify its industrial and technical/engineering characteristics, but also to assess the success of the plan under a commercial point of view. By doing so, it would be able to use moral suasion to "force" the developer to revisit a project that does not represent an attractive opportunity under a market perspective or that has low chances of completion unless some corrective actions are taken. In this way the bank would be acting on one side on the probability of default of the borrower, and on the other on the loss given default (or on the "cure rate") in case of failure of the project.

Consider the case of a real estate developer who finds himself out of funds before being able to complete a project for which he has received financing. Under these circumstances, the lender could decide to either pursue legal action against him in order to recover part of his credit, or agree to extend further funding, conditionally on the fact that the borrower revisits the characteristics of the project and acts in a disciplined way. In the first case, the chances of recovery are low, as the borrower is in financial distress and usually unable to sell the real estate assets as her/his development is not yet completed. Moreover, even if once the borrower has defaulted the bank were able to seize the property, the value it could derive from this collateral would likely be low. On the other hand, granting additional credit while imposing strong covenants and redirecting the developer towards projects that are either more feasible or more aligned to current market requests, can enable the bank to initially increase its exposure, incurring in more risk, but then it could me it be able to recover the whole amount lent once the project is successfully completed and the sales of the real estate are well received by the market (may be supported by generous mortgage offerings).

A third category of real estate assets that has to be considered is then constituted by all the properties that represent a guarantee to NPLs. In this case we are back to the realm of collateral assets: their relevance for the bank comes from the fact that in case of default of the borrower, those assets may become part of the category of repossessed assets that it ends owning. Due to the broad range of loans that characterize the activity of a bank, these assets are not necessarily commercial or residential real estate properties. For example, in the case of a corporate loan, the collateral may be represented by an industrial real estate property, while in the aforementioned case of a loan to a real estate developer, if the project is interrupted at a very early stage, a bank may find itself owning a brownfield (e.g. a field with a licence to build something in future but with no real estate as such).

A fourth category of real estate assets that the bank as to deal with are those that are managed by the bank on behalf of the clients. The ownership of the asset

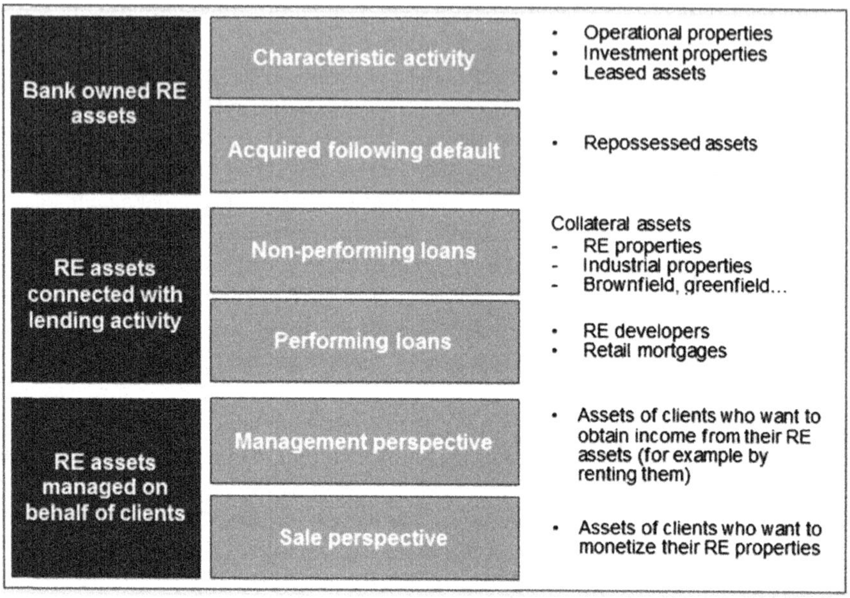

Fig. 9.1 Banking and real estate: intertwined businesses. Real estate assets managed by banks. *Source* Internal analysis

formally remains in the hands of the clients, as part of a larger investment portfolio, or as an asset that is related to some asset management or life insurance products. Clearly this is a wealth management service that does not imply at all that the mentioned real estate assets has any relationship with the bank's balance sheet, if not in an indirect way. But for the sake of completeness, it is worth to keep in mind even this last category to have the most accurate and holistic view of the above mentioned interconnections (see Fig. 9.1).

These examples show that the potential real estate "owned" or directly/indirectly managed by a bank can reach a significant weight within the bank's balance sheet. This is why after having focussed on the interrelations between real estate and banks, in the next section we develop an organized framework for the optimal management of the entire value chain that a bank could consider in order to actively manage the potential risks and returns coming from this asset typology.

9.3 An Optimal Management of Real Estate Assets

The optimal management of real estate assets can be performed following five different approaches or "enablers/accelerators" (see Fig. 9.2). These are not to be considered as alternatives to be implemented independently from one another, but as complementary set of actions that aim at different objectives and that have a

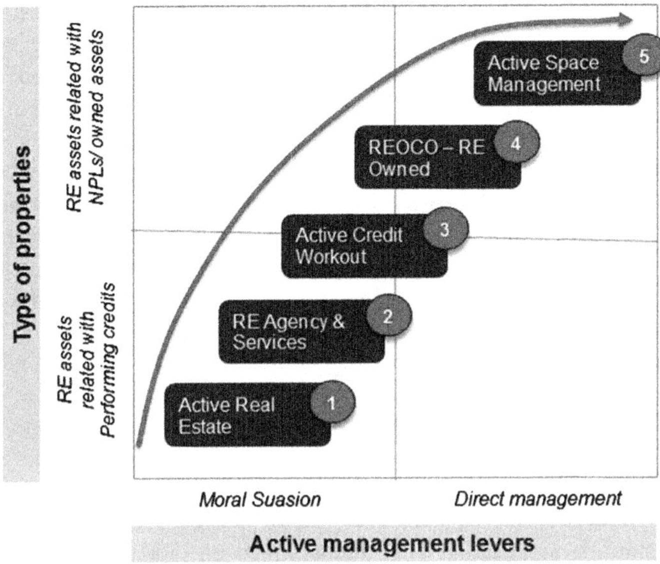

Fig. 9.2 Active management levers for real estate. Active management levers. *Source* Internal analysis

different effectiveness depending on the specific status of the underlying asset. In fact, as we have already discussed, the extent to which a bank can intervene on a real estate collateral depends in great part upon whether it is the legal owner or not. In the first case, a bank can directly act on the asset, while in the second its powers are limited to moral suasion. Although under some circumstances even simple moral suasion may allow to have a significant impact on the management of the asset, it is clear that the range of options available in case of a direct ownership is just not comparable. This is why there is a need for differentiating the optimal strategy depending on the more or less "direct" ownership of the asset: the aforementioned five approaches aim at doing so, and are logically divided depending on the management levers available to a bank at different times, as shown in the matrix below.

The first model, defined Active Real Estate Management (AREM), is implemented when loans are still performing, and hence the bank is obviously not the owner of the underlying asset. The AREM refers to a proactive approach in the holistic management of a real estate development backed loans portfolio: it is not a solution to a specific situation of distress, but rather an early monitoring tool for the critical situations that may be related to the different credit exposures of a bank towards real estate developers. Due to its relevance in acting as a preventive measure, rather than being simply a solution to a contingent problem, the AREM approach requires constant attention to the development and performance of the underlying collaterals to the portfolio. A specific section in this chapter will explain the main steps required for its designing and implementation.

A second action that can be carried out while loans are still performing, is helping borrowers in managing their real estate assets (financed by the bank), offering them intermediation (e.g. sales) services. In fact, a better execution of the sale of a given real estate collateral is essential in assessing the possible recovery rate of a credit, because its value impacts both the probability of default of a borrower and the cure rate in case of default. In this sense, a real estate agency service actually has a twofold role. At a first level, it may increase the chances of repayment of borrowers whose credits are still performing by helping them in obtaining better contractual conditions when trying to rent or sell their properties and offering lower fees for these services compared with traditional real estate agency services. On a second level, it may act as an accelerator enabling a bank to dispose of its repossessed real estate assets at higher prices or better conditions: in fact, a bank owned real estate agency would have a great access to a variety of marketing channels that are typically unavailable to a traditional bank and also could support the sale process by offering generous financing terms to entice the demand and help close the transaction.

The third model considered is the active credit workout—not a tool "per se", but rather an approach for dealing with credits which are not performing. Its scope covers therefore collateral assets which need to be recovered in some way to make up for the default of their respective loans. For this recovery, the choice of whether a judicial strategy is preferable to an out-of-court workout, and of whether the bank is better off outsourcing rather than managing internally its position has to take into account several issues, as already discussed in previous chapters. We just recall that when setting up a workout unit, a bank has to consider different dimensions, and most notably it needs to identify its best organizational set up, and the way it will deal with the ownership of the assets.

The fourth model considered refers to the acquisition of assets underlying non performing credits through a REOCO (Real Estate Owned Company). This structure has been already analyzed when discussing the enablers of a workout unit: in this sense, the role of the REOCO is to acquire real estate properties during auctions and to then play an active part in the management of such repossessed assets. The activity of the REOCO contributes to the build up of a real estate "hard assets" portfolio owned directly by the bank, and enables it to reach the critical mass that may be required in order to set up a structure that relies on the management of large volumes of assets in order to improve its efficiency. The REOCO is most effective when implemented in conjunction with a bank-owned real estate agency service. In fact, in this case there exist clear synergies between the two accelerators that can be exploited in order to increase their value. This shows that, as already mentioned, no action has to be evaluated under a standalone perspective as the final goal is to combine the different models to develop a holistic approach to real estate management.

Finally, the Active Space Management (ASM) approach marks the transition towards definitively becoming a professional player active throughout the real estate value chain. Through the active space management program a bank has to critically review the full range of properties it owns and define the optimal management strategy for each of them, possibly developing innovative solution aimed at maximizing their value. In the next section we will develop the concept, providing insight on some of the possible initiatives that can be implemented under this framework.

9.4 AREM—Active Real Estate Management

As already mentioned, the Active Real Estate Management (AREM) approach comprises preliminary actions that the bank puts in place when the credit is formally still performing and the ownership of the collateral is far from being in the bank's hands (see Fig. 9.3). Therefore, this set of measures is built up with the main objective of acting pre-emptively in order to avoid a possible situation of distress or default on the credit side, rather than waiting and acting when the sickness is already manifested. The key point of this approach is finding a proper way to first

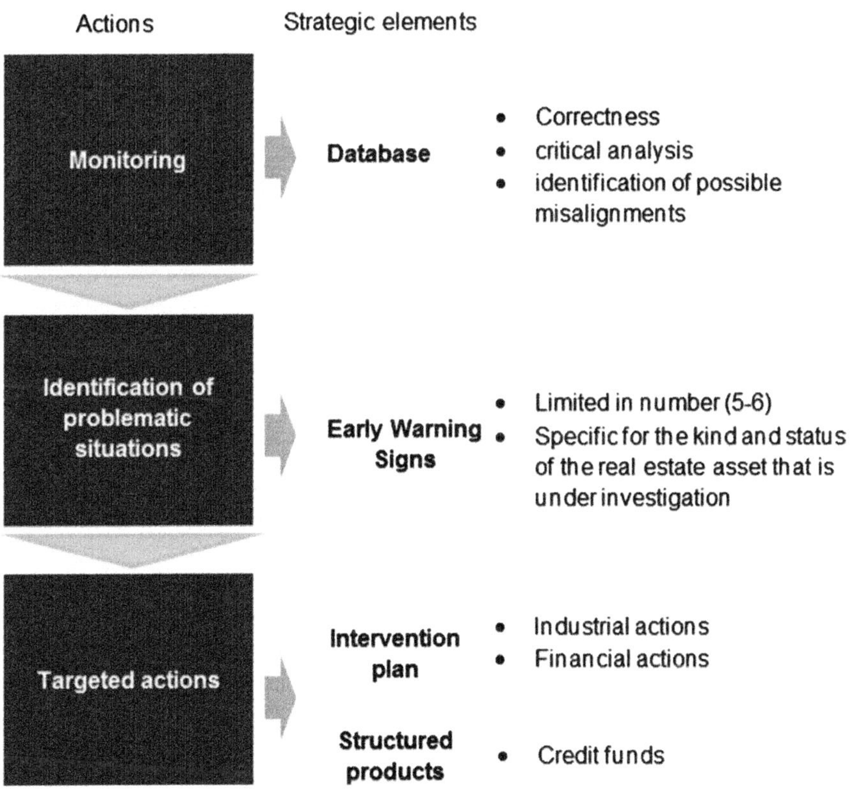

Fig. 9.3 From early warnings monitoring to targeted actions. Steps of active real estate management. *Source* Internal analysis

monitor the credit portfolio of the bank, and then identify which, among thousands of credits, are the ones that are likely to experience problematic situations, and finally implement the right moral suasion action aimed at avoiding, when it is possible, its default.

The first important step that must be implemented is a constant and targeted monitoring of the value of real estate assets underlying the credit positions on the bank's balance sheet. It is important to note that some of those assets will be already in place and ready to use, while others will be in much more uncertain situations, because—for example—they are still under construction. For the first category, the critical point is to identify the current value of the real estate asset and how this value could be destroyed. For the second category, the priority is to monitor the current status of construction and possibly to identify the factors that could hamper its completion (for example, funds are over when the building is only halfway through the construction phase) or that could bring the failure of the project (for example, close to completion, an important number of flats in a residential building under construction are not yet rented or sold, given a weak market demand).

The most important step when monitoring a large portfolio of loans which are all very different for what concerns the characteristics of the collateral is to then set up a database that cathegorizes all the real estate assets. This database has to be targeted and very specific, containing all the relevant technical, urbanistic, economic, and commercial information concerning the real estate assets to which the bank is indirectly exposed—everything the bank needs to know on their evolving value!

Once again, similarly as when we were talking about setting up a database for NPLs, the relevant and necessary information must be identified. Example of these elements and characteristics about the collaterals are: the kind of real estate asset (residential, office, retail, logistic); their status (new and ready to use, to be re-furbished, under construction); their location: where the asset is situated—big distinction if it is in or outside a main city or town; its covenants in favor of the bank or other parties; its valuation, possibly including date and valuation methods used; its regulatory status; its legal status; its current renting contracts, when outstanding and their current and projected yield.

Clearly, the adequacy of the database is determined by the completeness and quality of the data available, by the soundness of the valuation (particularly when referring to projects still under development) and by its volatility through time, as the value may change significantly over time.

When assessing the quality and reliability of a real estate database it is therefore important to focus on three main elements. Firstly, one must ensure that the information collected is not only correct, but also complete and updated. More specifically, there are some areas in which there is empirical evidence that the data is often missing, irrelevant, incorrect, or not updated. These areas are indications on the value and surface of the asset, technical and legal identifications, and physical assessment. The set of information collected has to be subsequently critically analyzed. This involves benchmarking its value with simple market parameters, when available, as price per square meter or average yield obtained by its renting. In a parallel way, a critical analysis must be performed to assess the strength of the main hypothesis underlying the business plan of a project under development, compared to the status quo: for example, a key metric to consider is the percentage of the whole asset that has been sold or pre rent. Finally, a bank must consider and value possible technical and building problems and assess how critical they are or could become.

The active monitoring effort has then to be reviewed at frequent intervals, prioritizing the positions characterized by a high loan to value and exposure. In order to identify the possible distressed situations on which the bank should preventively act, a set of Early Warning Signs (EWS) must be determined and implemented. The aim of those indicators is to anticipate, with a good degree of certainty, those situations that correspond to a deterioration of the credit quality. The EWS must be limited in quantity (usually 5–6 are enough), in order to ensure a focused analysis of the situation with no redundant information. Moreover, they have to be specific for the kind and status of the real estate asset that is under investigation. For example, in the commercial sector, EWS that would be meaningful are the percentage of vacancy, that ideally should not exceed 15 %, the maturity of the contracts, the cap rate, that is the total rent (ideally the cash inflows from the real estate asset) over the value of the building, its long term value, and its debt service ratio (that is, rents over debt).

When considering a residential development projects, the EWS that can be calculated and evaluated are the percentage of sold assets over the percentage of constructed ones (a good and healthy level is around 80–90 %), the percentage of maximum exposure used over the status of the project development (must be around 35 %), and its long term value. The EWS main value added is then in signaling the opportunity of activating proactive financial actions on loans that can be withdrawn, which may represent a significant part of total outstanding loans. Once the early wanings analysis have shown which are the most troubled situations, corrective actions with direct impact on the profit and loss of the counterpart must in fact be carried out. Those actions have to be focused on those loans that show a critical situation and give signals of a possible future default and that are of large enough value that the cost of actions would be covered and as such worthwhile.

Generally, specific action plans are designed on an ad hoc basis for loans of important dimensions, while proceduralized (or "industrialized") for smaller loans (see Fig. 9.4). The kind of actions that can be implemented are then both financial and industrial. Financial actions are taken on those loans that can be withdrawn when the EWS deteriorate and without any specific legal or financial risk. Those are aimed at limiting the bank's exposure to the client's default. Industrial actions are instead chosen when there is a development project that the owner has specific interests to take to completion (for example, he owns a construction company that would complete the works—and would face the risk of distress in case it should not be able to do so), and the real estate asset could have a reasonable market demand if properly reconsidered and maybe partially redesigned.

The corrective actions have to be rightfully prioritized and carefully evaluated in order to determine the effective chances on the repayment's chances and the

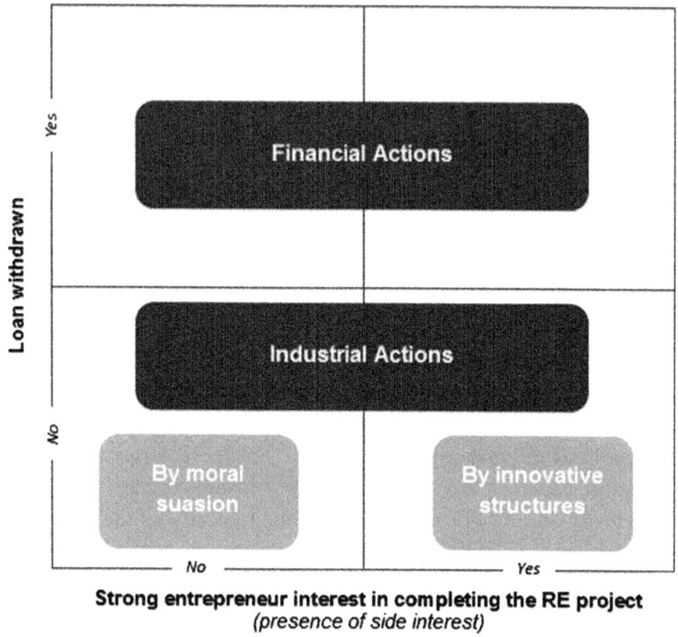

Fig. 9.4 Industrial and financial actions on subperforming loans. Industrial and financial actions. *Source* Internal analysis

potential broader impacts on the final customer. For what concerns the industrial actions, specific technical and specialist skills must be managed by the bank even if the basis for its intervention is just limited to moral suasion. Examples of Industrial moral suasion may involve for example the redesign of the overall structure of the project—e.g. to seek more efficiency and a better usage of space, changing the purpose of the asset in order to increase the cash inflows and therefore the repayment probability, or optimizing the usage of the remaining resources. Property management actions could instead be finalized at creating liquidity and maximizing the value generated from the sale of the real estate assets. Facility management actions could then be required to maintain the asset in a proper and workable state.

Finally, other Active Real Estate Management actions may deal with the origination with new sources or structures for the financing of the development project. New structured product solutions could, for example, involve the incorporation of a closed-end investment fund to which the bank can transfer its credits (see Fig. 9.5). The immediate advantage of this approach is that the bank does not have to sell the credits at discount, but it can sell them for a value close to the accounting value in exchange of financial instruments (and therefore reducing the negative impact of a loss on its tier 1 capital). A single or multiple sub-performing loans could therefore be contributed to a credit fund at their fair value and in the assumption of their going concern, in exchange for the related equity tranches. The credit fund would then be managed by a SPV that could in turn mandate specific restructuring advisers

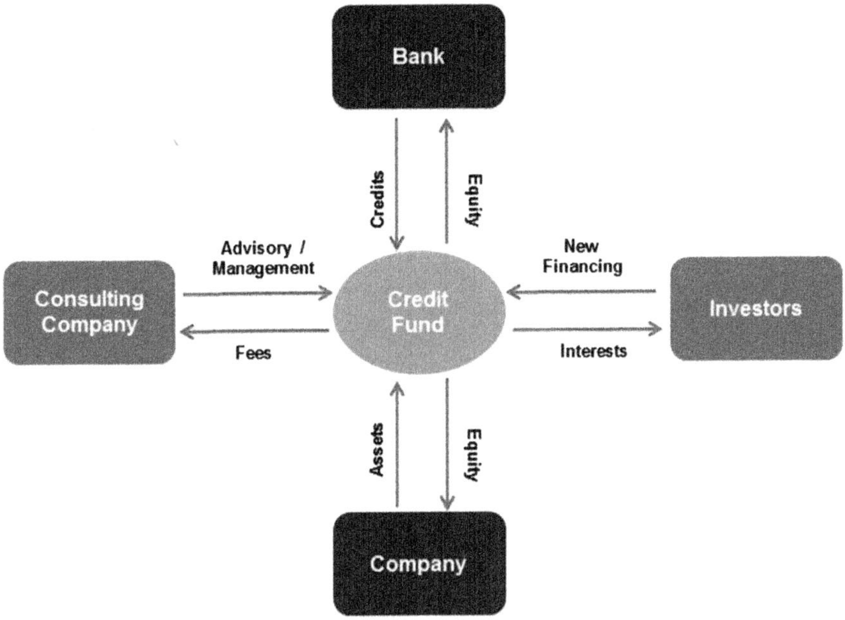

Fig. 9.5 Active managed credit fund: a possible structure. Credit fund scheme and participants. *Source* Internal analysis

to help dealing with one or more of the dossier. Investors get shares of the fund along with the bank that converts part of its loans into equity. The basic structure of the credit fund and the exchange of resources among the bank, the fund and the investors are shown in Fig. 9.5.

9.5 Active Space Management

Active Space Management is the last set of actions that can be implemented in order for the bank to actively and properly manage the portfolio of real estate assets that it directly owns (see Fig. 9.6). Therefore, differently from the AREM approach we previously discussed, we are now dealing with owned assets which the bank can directly manage, and with a view of maximizing their yield.

The aim of Active Space Management (ASM) is in fact to increase the productivity of those assets, maximizing the output given the inputs employed and through different potential initiatives—the maximization of the productivity ratio could be either achieved by maximizing the output obtained or by minimizing the input used. By firstly taking into consideration the input, ASM must act in order to rationalize or reduce the cost of the real estate assets the bank uses for its own uses.

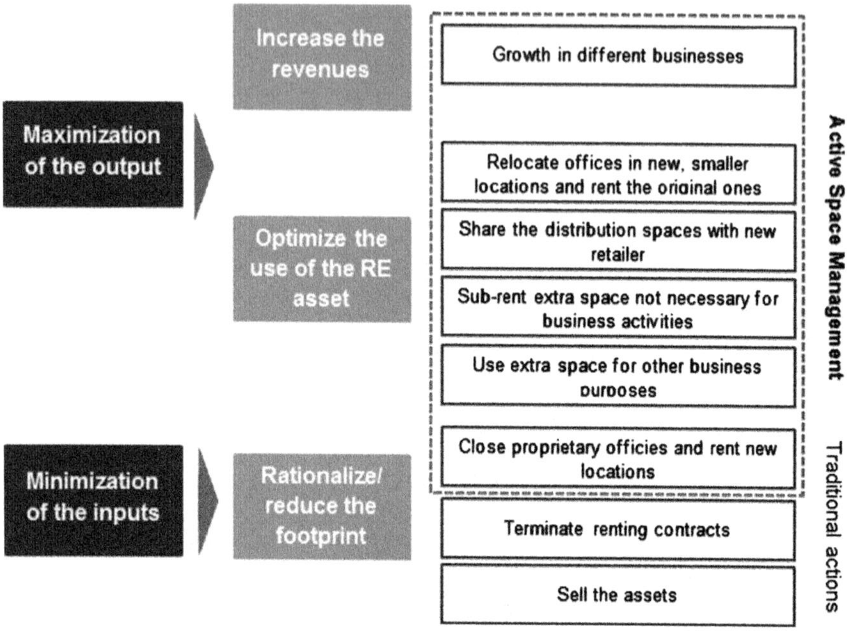

Fig. 9.6 Active space management to increase productivity. Exemplification of the active space management approach. *Source* Internal analysis

This can be achieved by selling property assets or by renegotiating its renting contracts. On the output side, the maximization can be achieved either by increasing the revenues obtained (e.g. by relocating the properties) or by optimizing the usage of the real estate assets owned. Revenues can be maximized for example by expanding the range of businesses in which to operate, obtaining high diversification. Concerning a better usage of the real estate asset, many actions can be taken. All of them are finalized at optimizing the existing space and finding a way to earn out more. Generally, this can be done by reallocating the space to different purposes, by moving offices to different locations in order to earn higher rents on the original spaces, by optimizing the available space, or by sub renting the locations when some room is not currently used. Figure 9.6 summarizes how an ASM approach can take place and exemplify what kind of actions can be implemented.

9.6 The Bank as an Integrated Real Estate Player

An integrated real estate approach allows a bank to act both on its cost of risk and on its profitability. With respect to the first area, we have illustrated how implementing an AREM approach can allow to detect troublesome situations and act on them to reduce their probability of default and the overall level of loss given default.

Similarly, accelerators such as a bank-owned real estate agency and a REOCO can allow to improve the situation of the borrower or to maximize the value that can be extracted from the collateral of a loan in case of default. Having said that, an integrated real estate approach impacts a bank's economic statement in ways that go beyond the simple benefits that can be achieved through cost of risk reduction. It is indeed true that optimizing the recovery value leads to positive effects on earnings. On one side, reducing the probability of default of a borrower and restoring his financial situation makes it possible for a bank to continue to earn the interest income on the loan, which would be foregone in case of protracted distress of the counterparty. On the other hand, increasing recovery value in case of default allows it to limit the write offs that a bank would incur if it were to sell at a high discount or have a worthless property.

Besides increasing the recovery value on NPLs, and hence improving a bank's perspectives in terms of reduced need to write-off, an integrated real estate approach has positive impacts in other ways as well. In fact, the real estate platform allows a bank to position itself at the center of a network of services connected with real estate assets. If the system is well developed and efficient, providers of a disparate range of real estate related services will have an incentive to rely on the bank and its distribution channels, be it branches or online networks, in order to gain access to potential customers. The bank could then request fees for its intermediation role and secure a new source of income. As shown in Fig. 9.7, a bank could follow a customer throughout the whole process of acquiring a property, from the initial

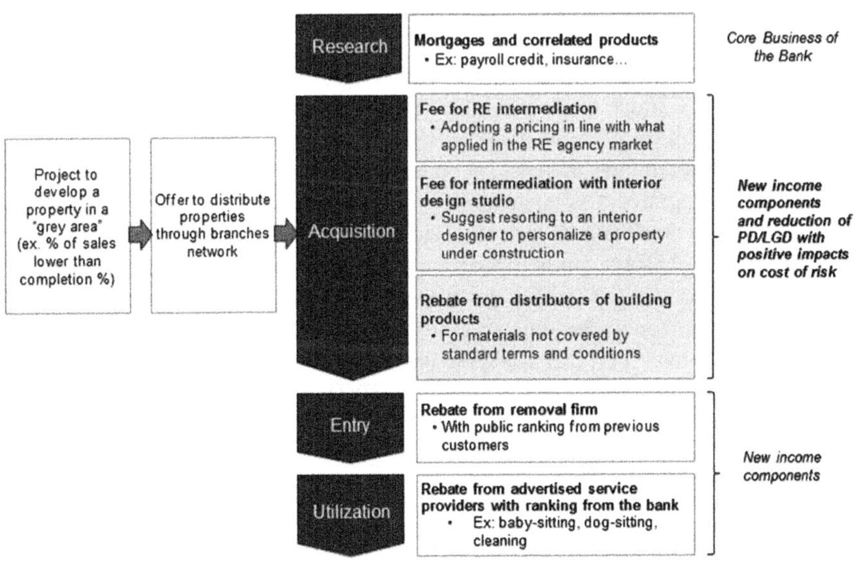

Fig. 9.7 Bank's potential roles along the value chain. Impact on the income statement of the bank. *Source* Internal analysis

stage of its search to its financing to the actual utilization and resell phase. At each level, it would be possible to extract different kinds of fees (see Fig. 9.7).

Under an integrated real estate framework, the profitability of each mortgage can significantly increase, because the loan works as a "hook product" that can capture fees from a whole range of additional activities. These cover a broad spectrum, from simple real estate intermediation fees to provision of services connected with the maintenance of the asset (for example property and facility management), to the focused cross selling of correlated products (for example theft insurance and security services). A bank can hence increase its offer with high value added products and services related to the real estate assets. This also allows to potentially capture a higher market share in the segment of "high quality" mortgages: in fact, borrowers in this sector are less price sensitive, and they are likely willing to pay more in order to obtain a comprehensive service. In the case of retail clients, this would potentially mean offering advisory support from the phase of research of the property to the management of the administrative process connected with the purchase, and acting as a platform through which customers can access all collateral services as well.

In the case of small enterprises, a bank could make its real estate properties available to the firm in order to support the development or restructuring of the business through actions on the real estate assets. All the above mentioned activities can provide an additional source of revenues and at the same time they most likely do not entail major structural changes for the bank. In fact, a bank already has a pool of trained resources and of infrastructures than can be leveraged with this aim. Moreover, its brand name can help it in addressing trust issues that are critical in the real estate sector. This means that through the limited reconversion of people and with the leverage of existing physical and IT infrastructure, it may be able to address the needs of an integrated real estate platform. A bank owned real estate agency can also provide an additional positive externality. Since customers would be able to find in a single location all the services related to the acquisition of a real estate property, under a one-stop-shop framework, the flow of customers in the branches could potentially increase, supporting the acquisition of new clients.

Finally, an integrated real estate approach can help increase the value of the real estate portfolio that a bank "controls"—either directly or indirectly, as explained. On one hand the platform can help a bank revamp and dispose of the assets that are no longer core for its business. On the other, it may allow to sell the properties of a client that can no longer be able to face interest payments on his loan, or find attractive exit options for a real estate development that is entering in a "grey area".

Chapter 10
The WHAM of a Troubled Leasing Equipment Portfolio

Abstract Leasing is a peculiar component of the overall credit portfolio of a bank—even more so for a NPLs portfolio as the assets being financed are already directly owned by the bank and therefore even more apt to a holistic and active management to realize their best exit value. However, direct ownership poses also a number of potential operational and reputational risks that needs to be monitored and addressed by the credit work out managing them in the best interest of the bank. Also, some kind of assets (e.g. equipment) have got steep decay curves and tend to loose their value quickly, if not actively managed and brought to market quickly and through the best channels. The remarketing strategy of leasing assets is therefore a crucial component to be addressed and requires a strong data set, well developed value decay functions and multiple distribution channels.

Keywords Leasing portfolio · Collaterals · Short term actions · Leasing value creation · Real estate leasing

10.1 The Management of an NPL Leasing Portfolio

This chapter focuses on a specific kind of NPLs portfolios, e.g. those connected with leasing assets, and will discuss the best strategies that can be implemented in order to actively deal with them. This category of NPLs has some peculiarities—related to the fact that the asset is already owned by the bank. It follows that accelerated losses of the intrinsic and market value of the assets related to the leasing finance are quite a critical issue for the balance sheets of most European banks. When trying to sell these assets, banks face a double problem: on one side, the difficult economic situation has made the sale process increasingly longer, leading to the need of a mounting level of provisions; on the other, a depressed market situation means that the sale often takes place at prices that are lower than the face value, leading to losses whose net present value is higher than the accounting value of the provisions recorded. Given the situation, banks should

C. Scardovi, *Holistic Active Management of Non-Performing Loans*,
DOI 10.1007/978-3-319-25363-3_10

identify new ways to manage leasing portfolios, especially those linked to NPLs, in order to reduce their negative economic impact.

In this chapter we suggest two approaches for doing so: the first is a short term initiative, aimed at remarketing leased assets underlying NPLs portfolios in order to achieve immediate results. The second approach is instead a medium-long term program focused on their real estate underlying: we will highlight how an AREM strategy can be applied to the biggest asset classes in the leasing portfolios, improving the balance sheet situation in the long run.

10.2 Leasing: It's All About the Underlying

When analyzing the credit risk linked to leasing contracts, great attention must be paid on the underlying of the contract itself. In fact, in a leasing contract a bank is from inception the legal owner of it (even if the lessee actually has the full use of such asset). It follows that when a lessee is unable to pay, the bank can take immediate repossession and direct action on it. This is why any strategy related with leased assets, be it short or long term, cannot disregard the specificities of the collateral. The relevant distinctions in this sense have been already analyzed when discussing the main drivers in portfolio valorization. In that context, we carried out an analysis of the factors that affect a collateral and its market value, starting from the status of the company which is currently using it, its transfer costs, the number of potential buyers and their geographical location. We also stressed that besides considering these macro-elements, one must take into account the category to which the asset belongs (real estate, energy, auto, industrial goods, maritime etc.).

In fact, this determines in turn the speed at which the collaterals loose value (as per their different decay curves) and consequently the degree of urgency that has to be attributed to the sale of different assets. Moreover, depending on the category to which they belong, collaterals entail different profiles in terms of marketability. Besides the fact that it has an evident financial impact on the recovery perspectives of a bank, the underlying is important for other reasons as well. In fact, there may be other significant risks connected with the fact that the bank is the actual owner of the asset. Specifically, the bank could be held responsible for the damages that may derive from its negligence in managing the collateral. Leasing portfolios can hence create a new source of complexity: they entail operational and reputational risks besides the "traditional" costs associated with credit risk: the bank could face additional expenses connected to the potential liability costs. Moreover, operational risk is not limited to economic terms: in fact, liabilities related with leased assets could also have a reputational impact on the bank. The extent of this risk is very much dependent on the nature of the underlying asset. For example, it could be incredibly high for some sorts of industrial equipments that can cause environmental damage if not properly maintained (e.g. a chemical plants), while the issue may be less relevant for more standard collaterals.

10.3 Short Term Management Actions on Leasing NPL

In this section, we focus on short term actions that are primarily focused at efficiently re-marketing the collateral assets that are underlying a leasing NPLs portfolio. We start by highlighting how the optimal strategy can vary depending on the class to which the asset belongs (real estate, energy, auto, industrial goods, maritime); we then move to discuss the existing options in terms of distribution channels. Finally, we suggest a work plan to implement these actions in a pragmatic way. In fact, the major differences in terms of marketability among the different assets categories make it necessary to design a customized marketing plan for each of them. This has to be tailored to the characteristics of the underlying good: adopting a one-size-fits-all approach is not an effective solution, because it does not allow to exploit the synergies that can be derived from the specificities of each asset and from the interaction among the different structures of a workout framework.

This concept will become clearer by analyzing the optimal marketing structure for a real estate leasing. In this case, the bank has probably a great extent of expertise and knowledge about the underlying, and even more so if it has established a real estate management structure such as the one discussed in the previous chapter. In this case it possible to leverage on the bank owned real estate agency service to help the sales of real estate assets in a more effective and economical way. The main activities that can be undertaken in this regard are summarized in Fig. 10.1.

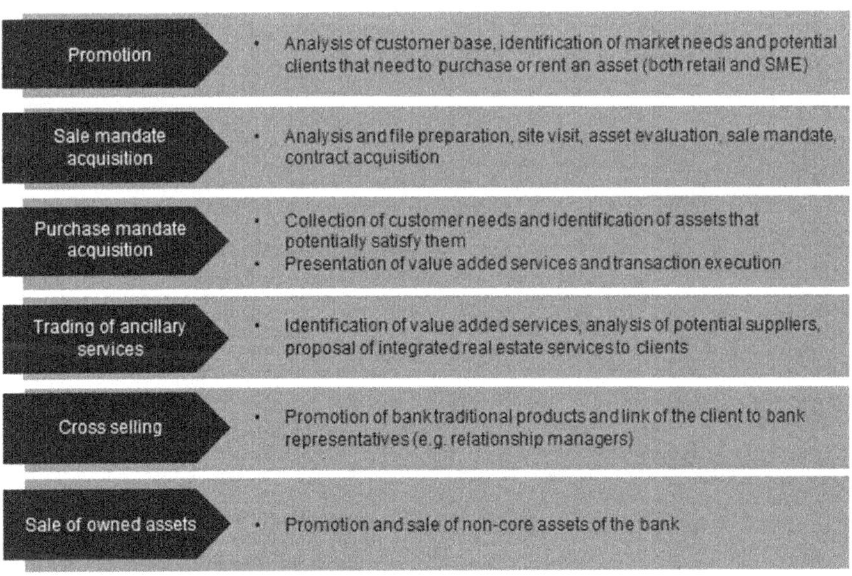

Fig. 10.1 Main activities to leverage real estate intermediation. Main activities of a RE agency. *Source* Internal analysis

Some of the listed actions, such as trading of ancillary services and cross selling, already go beyond a simple re-marketing activity: in fact they potentially allow to extract additional fees and capture new business. This is in line with the overall goal of an active workout: action is not passive and limited to simple recovery, but aimed at maximizing value by implementing innovative ideas.

The same concept can be applied when discussing about renewable energy related infrastructure leasing. In this case, under a baseline strategy, the underlying assets could be sold to either financial investors or industrial players in the same sector that are willing to expand their capacity and consolidate the market. An alternative approach would be to act to make the renewable energy plant viable and economic again. This presumably entails a great degree of effort: when a company stops fulfilling its lease payments it usually means that the stage of distress it is experiencing is severe, as the utilization of the leased assets is fundamental for carrying out their operating activity.

Nevertheless, especially if supported by the investors of the company, a bank could push for a restructuring of the business in order to enable the lessee to gain sufficient funding to fulfill its contractual obligations. In the case of leased vehicles, marketing can take different forms depending on the type of asset—whether it is a commercial, industrial or city vehicle, as summarized (see Fig. 10.2).

The re-marketing and sale of industrial equipment requires that the assets are properly described: goods in this category are in fact very heterogeneous, and hence each of them requires a set of specific information. Besides general information that is relevant for any kind of good (year of construction, manufacturer, model, serial number, current location) one must take into account a range of additional characteristics, which change depending on the underlying. For example, in the case of construction equipment, the residual value is greatly impacted by its conditions and the number of hours for which it has been in operation, while key aspects for

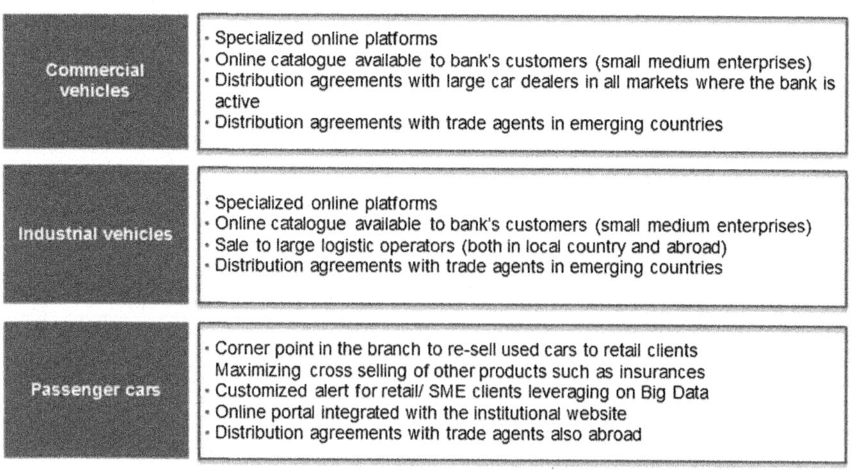

Fig. 10.2 Re-marketing strategy for different vehicles. *Source* Internal analysis

assessing the recovery potential on a press machine are its press force, plate size and type of feeder. Due to the high specificity of some of these assets, in order to market them, besides resorting to the generic distribution channels a bank may have in place, it could be possible to leverage on existing online platforms for specific asset classes—many are operated by independent players.

Finally, for what concerns maritime leasing, repossessed yachts and recreational ships can be managed in different ways. While sale through a specialized operator is obviously possible, a bank may also offer them to its private, affluent clients without the need of external advisors and agents. This can potentially be done through a dedicated portal and selected marketing campaigns. Alternatively, a bank may choose to export the assets to emerging economies through selected trade agents. If the pool of assets in this category were very large, an innovative solution could entail the creation of a charter company that could finance itself through the temporary rent of ships.

As it can be seen, different asset categories are associated with different distribution channels, as well as marketing strategies, that need to be identified for each of them. With respect to information and distribution channels, a bank can rely on both internal and external platforms. On one hand, it can develop its own online network for some assets, leverage its corporate branches for others and resort to leasing companies in foreign markets to find alternative lessees. On the other, for assets with a greater level of specificity, it may leverage on equipment manufacturers, industry associations or external re-selling platform. There exist a multitude of specialized players in this field: some companies buy and directly resell formerly leased assets, while others simply limit their scope of action to managing previously leased NPLs assets as brokers. Mutual agreements with other banks in foreign markets can also be considered, in order to access countries where the bank does not have a direct presence. An heterogeneous geographical market mix is indeed another aspect that should be taken into account. For example, for some assets it may be worth targeting countries with specific industries that are significantly growing or that are willing to invest to increase their production capacity. It could also be possible to sell in emerging markets, through partnerships with importers or international branches of the bank.

10.4 A Medium-Long Term Program for Real Estate Leasing Contracts

Apart from short term programs, also a number of medium-long term ones could be considered. In this chapter we will focus and discuss the ones related to the management of real estate assets. Again, as we have already highlighted in the previous chapter, our suggested approach is what we have dubbed "Active Real Estate Management" (AREM). This approach takes into consideration both the balance sheet value and the income generation potential of real estate assets serving as collateral for loans (in this case leasing—e.g. where the real estate is already owned by the bank).

The process applied to leasing contracts does not differ too much from what we described when talking in general about the AREM: it is developed through three main steps that are monitoring, identifying critical situation, and applying corrective actions, mostly in an indirect way and through moral suasion. The monitoring has to be periodical and based on an accurate database. It is specifically targeted at identifying, through the help of limited but highly effective means as early warning signals, those situations in which the property status could potentially become critical. An early identification is the key for the success of the initiative. When critical situations are promptly identified and analysed, the proper corrective actions can then be planned and timely implemented. These actions can have financial nature, or, most importantly in the case of leasing, industrial.

In any case, they are aiming at maximizing the possible recovery value. Within the AREM approach, the identification of those positions that, even if not yet defaulted, are still at high risk of loss is therefore of primary importance. Clearly, the positions on which the bank risks the most are those that, independently from the exposure, have high or very high loan to value. For them it becomes even more important the set up of targeted corrective actions with medium-long term impacts, usually involving three activities (asset, property and facility management) as already discussed in previous chapters. Apart from these mid-long term activities, others could be carried out via a crash program (see Fig. 10.3). After the asset values have been checked, the priorities among them have to be identified. The bank has to determine which situations can be handled internally and which ones by industry experts and then it may have to design industrial projects to manage the

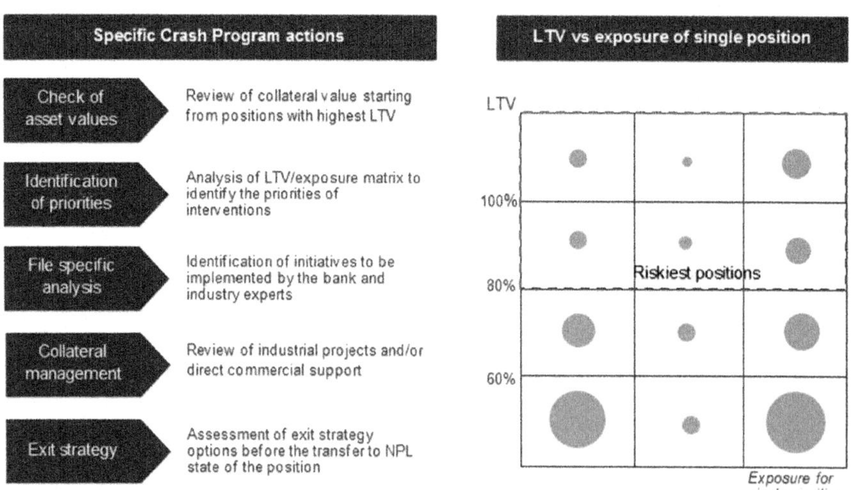

Fig. 10.3 The five steps of a crash program. Crash program designed to efficiently deal with the bank's riskiest leasing positions. *Source* Internal analysis

collateral. Finally an exit strategy has to be identified in order to extract value from the position.

Since the real estate collateral in leasing contracts could be of different types, it is important that the corrective actions are rightfully tailored in order to optimally deal with the different situations—e.g. considering that the likelihood of success of a corrective action depends on the destination of use and on the location of the asset (e.g. residential or commercial building will be much easier to handle than industrial, land or development projects—at green or brown field stage).

10.5 Value Creation in Leasing

As we have previously specified, leasing contracts bear many risks and disadvantages for the bank: among the others, the fact that the bank is the owner of the collateral asset and therefore it may bear a number of other legal and reputational risks connected with the assets leased, usually very heterogeneous in nature (from a real estate property, to a car or boat, to any other piece of equipment). Therefore, given that the leasing market is characterized by slow growth, increasing regulation, limited profitability and high risk, it is important to be able to identify what could be the drivers that could potentially help the bank in creating value from its leasing operations. Those drivers aim at addressing the main weaknesses of the sector and turn them into strengths and are mainly related to the holistic and active management of the leasing underlying assets to the leasing.

Firstly, a better credit quality should be targeted also starting from the commercial policies designed and followed by the bank. Starting with its planning, the bank should focus on identifying the credit allocation that it could allow it to optimize the trade off between diversification (choosing leasing contracts across quite different and heterogeneous underlying being financed) and a focalization on those kind of collateral where it has more technical and industrial expertise. Single credit positions should then be adequately priced—given the specific underlying asset (not just looking at the riskiness of the counterpart being financed, but also looking at the kind of asset and at the opportunities of its re-marketing, should something go wrong with the original loan).

Of course, the single leasing contract should be analyzed in the context of the overall commercial relationship the client has with the bank. And pricing should be risk adjusted on the basis of the riskiness of the underlying and of the easiness of its re-marketing (in case the bank will need to repossess it and sell it to recover the value of the defaulted leasing contract). Indeed, we could argue that the quality of the underlying, and its value decay function through time are strongly driving the overall probability of default of the leasing and—even more importantly—its loss given default.

The maximization of the recoverable value is then targeted by proactive recovery strategies—partially similar to what we already discussed, that are driving active workout actions that will also allow to the bank to reduce its operating and reputational risks. As explained, a key element in the leasing business that has to be properly taken into account, evaluated and monitored through its lifetime is the underlying asset. It represents a source of risk for the bank, both in legal, reputational and economic/financial terms. However, it is also the main element that gives the bank the opportunity to create value as a basis for the commercial, pricing and remarketing decisions.

Chapter 11
Working It Out: From Value Recovery to Value Creation

Abstract Credit work out, as a science and as an art, has been rapidly evolving in the last few years in response to the global financial crisis that created unprecedented levels of NPLs in Europe. The most effective drivers of development have been the exploitation of new technologies and data management (e.g. in order to build predictive algorithms and comprehensive WHAM dashboards) but also the increasing "industrialization" of the approaches. Industrialization aims to bring new ideas and best practices from a number of different industries to increase the operational efficiency and it could allow few players to grow and consolidate the market, still very fragmented and sometimes quite inefficient and opaque. More broadly, the challenge of the credit work out industry could be in the next few years its shift in focus: from value recovery to value creation.

Keywords Credit workout evolution · Industrialization · Innovations · Holistic workout · Active workout

11.1 The Evolution of the Credit Work Out Business

In this last chapter we will briefly describe how two further macro levers could support and accelerate the development of the credit work out business into more mature stages, refocussing its main aim and mission from "value recovery" to "value creation" (e.g. enlarging the focus of its managerial actions from the optimization of the recovery index considered on its NPLs under management to the optimization of the return of the equity invested in the platform by its shareholders). Whilst the two further macro levers define a rough approximation and a brutal simplification of many other competitive actions that could be pursued to reach such a target, we believe they are characterizing well most of the evolutionary trends that can be observed at the level of the best practices in this specific and peculiar industry—in Europe and elsewhere.

C. Scardovi, *Holistic Active Management of Non-Performing Loans*,
DOI 10.1007/978-3-319-25363-3_11

Industrialization, the first lever, aims at making more efficient the overall work of the platform, mutualizing best practices and lessons learned (but also methodologies and experiences) coming from non financial industries. As much part of the credit work out activities are carried over a large number of NPLs to manage and involving a good number of repeatable activities, industrializing its core operating model could mean ensuring a more compelling cost to income, but also less reworking and a more uniform and higher standard of work and quality of services.

Innovation, the second lever, aims in turn at creating new sources of revenues, derived from adjacent businesses to the one of the credit recovery that can be obtained leveraging the most precious competitive components of credit work out. We believe that most of this critical components relate to the generation and ownership of better information and know how on the loans and underlying assets. We will then discuss options to consider to potentially open up interesting new ways of monetizing such information/know how advantages.

11.2 The Industrialization of Credit Recovery

While it is undeniable that the financial crisis shook up the business model and profitability profile of the global players in the financial sector, early warnings of the need for change in the banking sector could have be seen even before the events of 2008. Indeed, the crisis only contributed in exacerbating the problems that were already affecting the traditional banks, and specifically those related on one hand to threats coming from regulation and on the other to competition from either new entrants or new business models (e.g. competition from private funds which grant high yield credit to enterprises, being able to count on flexible cost structures; crowd funding initiatives that resort to the World Wide Web to gather capitals for start-ups and initiatives with a high level of technological content; non-banking firms offering financial advisory services at a lower price than what a traditional bank could offer etc.). Besides these first factors, banks have been increasingly exposed to the risk of disintermediation—which is partly becoming a necessity, because of the increased costs faced in their funding, given their ALM and higher capitalization requirements.

Part of such disintermediation risk (given the time mismatch) can then turn into liquidity risk and then in the insolvency of the counterparty. This has a double effect: on one side, it impacts the cost of credit for banks, which in turn reduces its rating and hence the costs it faces when gathering funds on the bond market, if not the very possibility of being able to access such markets; on the other, it expands the amount of NPLs in its balance sheet, which add up to their overall stock. This means that recovery costs and losses associated with NPLs are becoming even more critical.

With regards to the operating costs of the credit work out, both captive and independent units will then need to revise their costs structure, in order to maintain a decent level of profitability, transforming their somewhat "ad hoc" modus operandi into a more industrialized one. The objective of industrialization of the credit work out activities encompasses different aspects. First of all, it is driven by the need to optimize their cost structure, in order to become as flexible as possible, pushing the operating leverage as the workload can vary a lot through the economic cycle and be rather volatile also over short term periods. Secondly, it is also driven by a search for standardization and greater reliability that makes its core activities safer in the medium term. Thirdly, industrialization can push as well for an efficient redesign "front-to-back" of the main activities of the work out unit—it could thus optimize its productivity over time, maximizing the recovery rates that it can attain on the managed portfolios. Given the importance of industrialization in the workout process, we therefore briefly highlight the main principles and levers that a credit work out unit—either captive or non captive—should consider.

The key principles of industrialization are inspired by the mantra of minimizing the inputs (the costs incurred by the work out unit), whilst maximizing the output (the recovery rate, given the relevant benchmarks), at the same time improving the quality and reliability of the services provided (and by this way, reducing the operating risks normally attached to this kind of activities).

With respect to the target of input minimization, it is possible to improve efficiency in either the direct or indirect costs, sharing some of the investments with competitors or with industrial partners, or achieving economies of scale by expanding, aggregating or extending processes that have a significant component of fixed costs. In order to increase output, given the same inputs, and the quality and time to market of the services offered, the credit work out unit could instead increase the range of services offered through its own platforms (as discussed in the following paragraph), or the earnings it can achieve by systematically re-pricing its offering on the basis of its value added, but also taking into consideration the elasticity of the demand side of the competitive market equation. Finally, reducing the time to market of the recovery, especially in a situation when technological innovation is making underlying collateral (mainly equipment) even more rapidly obsolete, is another fundamental dimension that needs to be pursued and can be driven by the industrialization of the work out operating model. It is worth to summarize the main industrialization levers that could be considered and utilized in order to reshape and reorganize the overall operating model of the credit work out—five main drivers as explained in Fig. 11.1, each of which can be further analyzed by resorting to micro industrialization levers, as exemplified in the figure.

The first driver, the "servicing model" has as its main aim the increase of the productivity of the services offered by the credit work out to support the business development and target customers. This can be done by reducing cost redundancies, but also by pooling and sharing similar activities or platforms, allowing other services (sometimes born out of internal needs, such as reporting on the recovering activities) to be marketed to external parties for a fee (asset/capabilities marketability). Also the "internal marketplace" concept would allow to benchmark the internal costs related with any kind of scarce resources used for the activities carried out with what could be obtained externally and at market conditions. This continuos competitive benchmarking would increase transparency and incentivize a better

Industrialization levers		
Servicing model	**Pooling and sharing (infra-group)**	Creation of internal platforms to manage different divisions, to reduce overlapping, benefiting from scale economies, optimization and normalization of demand management
	Demand Management	Uniformation of purchases and elimination of wastes
	Internal Market	Creation of transparency on market value of internal activities and execution of comparative analysis
	Liquidation of resources/ competences	Transformation of production plants from cost centers into profit centers
Footprint model	**Right sharing**	Reallocation of the activities in order to optimize labor cost
	Ridefinition of Real Estate spaces	Cost and investment reduction by uniformation of Real Estate spaces to the operating strategy
Delivery model	**Outsourcing/ insourcing**	Cost reduction through externalization of activities/ exploitment of extra capacity by internalization of suppliers' activities
	Alliances	Partnership with third parties share investments and operating costs
Process excellence and organizational efficiency	**Front to back redesign**	Reorganization of the value chain and concentration of investments on key and value added phases
	Rationalization and standardization	Reduction of complexity by products, processes, procudures and systems standardization,
	Digitalization and automatization	Productivity boosting and operating costs reduction through technology
	Organizational restructuring	Cost reduction and more flexibility

Fig. 11.1 An industrialization framework. Industrialization levers. *Source* Internal analysis

performance and use of scarce resources. Similarly, the quality of the inputs required by the different divisions has to be monitored, and best providers among either internal divisions and external servicers have to be identified and continuously challenged sin order to prevent inefficiencies, wastes and cross subsidies (demand management).

The second driver is the "footprint model", which analyzes what is the best positioning for the manufacturing, distribution (e.g. regional collection network) and management units of the credit work out in "physical" terms (e.g. focusing on the real estate assets, and on the location of the premises of the work out). This implies first choosing the optimal location in which to operate, and subsequently detailing the specific type of properties where the operating and business units of the credit work out have to be positioned (real estate footprint redesign).

The third driver, the delivery model tries to ensure the optimal efficacy/efficiency of the execution of the main production and distribution phases, given the chosen competitive strategy. This translates into decisions with respect to the optimal level of outsourcing and insourcing of different functions, given on one end the relative performance of an internal unit with respect to the market average, and on the other end the level of strategic relevance of the activity performed. A closely related micro-lever that has to be considered is for example cost mutualization, which consists in evaluating the possibility of cooperation strategies, aimed at improving efficiency under a pool and share scheme that could be realized with either competitors or business partners.

The fourth driver, process excellence and organizational efficiency, acts on the simplification and standardization of the organization and processes of the credit work out, aiming at making them at the same time as relevant and incisive as possible. Depending on the specific situation this model can be implemented by resorting to different micro-levers. The "front-to back" and "rationalization and standardization" approaches imply a complete redesign of both manufacturing and distribution processes with the goal of simplifying them and reducing redundancies, making sure to identify which structures are suitable for maximum standardization and which are instead value drivers and hence should maintain specific characteristics. "Digitalization and automation" can also be applied pervasively throughout most of the activities of the credit work out: development of technology and of digital applications can both reduce costs of traditional procedures and help optimize some procedures that are instead typical of the traditional banking business. From an organizational standpoint, it is important to achieve both right sizing (in order to contain costs) and optimal design (developing a system with the proper number of reporting levels and hierarchical structure—setting a rather flat organization focused on the most effective/efficient recovery).

Lastly, the governance model examines how to structure the business and operating management of the credit work out, in order to maximize its degree of productivity and its proactivity in handling internal and external changes. Industrializing the decision making process could also lead to reducing its complexity and increasing its speed to recovery. Industrialization can mark a significant transition in the life of a credit work out: on one side it is necessary to ease this process, possibly by resorting to a "program management" micro-lever. On the other, a credit work out must make sure that all the efforts undertaken are effectively producing some results: productivity monitoring can help in making sure that the strategy is aligned to the pre-fixed objectives and that a proper intervention is considered if this is not the case. In any case, the transition cannot be limited to the work out as an entity, but has to encompass the culture of the people working for it, having employees feeling more involved in what they do, and adopting a more entrepreneurial attitude.

11.3 Innovations

A competitive credit work out (usually working according to a market proofed strategy and under a non captive governance frame) can develop skills and intelligence which can be leveraged for other purposes, in potentially quite profitable ways. Starting from the know how accumulated on the NPLs managed (segmented into homogeneous clusters as per the previous discussions on criteria to be considered), a credit work out could develop a number of adjacent services, offered to third parties for a fee that could involve value added services such as:

- Valuation and due diligence services on the loans and on their collaterals could be offered for a fee, basically using the same structured that the work out has to have anyway, although potentially with some level of conflict of interests with other adjacent activities that will be later discussed, and with the same "success fee/carried interest structure" that could be adopted to manage (at least partially) the compensation structure of the credit work out;
- Administrative and reporting services for the owners of the loans (the banks, or the financial investors) could also be offered, with tailored analysis on the evolution of the NAV (Net Asset Value) of the portfolios, given certain trends and behaviours of the macro risk/performance indicators. Again, most of the reporting and dashboard tools would be needed anyway by the credit work out, to ensure a proper and efficient management of the NPLs;
- Active management of the collateral, which is core to a strategy of optimal credit recovery, could also be sold for a fee to the third parties which are their indirect owner (or the direct ones, in case the NPLs are referred to non performing leasing contracts). For real estate assets, as seen, such services could comprise asset, property and facility management, and potentially extend to real estate agency services, for the collateral repossessed. Similar services could be offered for the management of equipment, maritime or other collaterals;
- For such collaterals, some P&C insurance coverage could also be cross sold, to mitigate the risks that such assets are still facing, even if partially unused and not yet repossessed. Other risk management structures—either standard or created ad hoc, above and beyond the most simple P&C coverage structures, could then address other macro risk factors, such as foreign exchange or interest rate

volatility—they could severely impact through time the value of the collateral and therefore the cure rate and LGD of the related loan;

- Structuring and slicing portfolios for their best sale could also be an adjacent advisory activity offered for a fee by a credit work out unit. Such support to the origination and closing of a sale transaction could involve either a "high touch" approach (e.g. senior advisors involved in the analysis of the portfolios, on their structuring and in their best sales strategy, directly negotiating with the demand-side counterparts) or a "high tech" approach that would rely mainly on the digital marketplaces already active for such kind of assets;
- The definition of recovery indexes, highly objective, robust and independently created (and therefore credible to third party investors) could also represent a new development for the best credit work outs (by definition, few indexes can really become the "golden rule" of the market), potentially generating very few fees, but also a quite valuable market recognition. Once such indexes on the recovery rates for the main clusters are available, hedging structures (either in the form of total return swaps, or as financial insurance guarantees) could then be operated effectively and with a good degree of liquidity and transparency. And the credit work out could become part of such a scheme, as the broker/dealer, in connection with other investment banks or credit insurance companies for the matching of the hedging contracts being created and for the placement of the risks undertaken.

These are just few of the examples of "diversification by adjacencies" that could improve the overall profitability of the platform and its "marketability" as a potentially good investment for private investors. Of course, any new addition to the core business of the recovery should be gauged against the further complexity which is contributing to the overall management of the company and to the risk of making the strategic intent of the company more unfocussed and its marketing message to potential clients, investors and employees. Also, great care should be considered in relation to the potential conflicts of interests vis a vis the "core" credit recovery activity and to the potentially increased level of operational and reputational risks attached to them.

11.4 Working It Out: Holistic and Active

Both the industrialization and the innovation of the credit work out business and operating model are indicating a potentially disruptive way forward for the credit work out units now operating at "full speed" (and often in a very traditional way), given the backlog left after the great financial crisis that started in 2008. It should be noticed however that the perspective of "value creation" for the shareholders of the work out could be linked back in a very direct and powerfull way to its "value recovery capacity". In fact, given the appropriate incentive structure, the mission of a credit work out is not dissimilar to the one of a professional private investors, that invests big money in order to get some gain (carried interest) out of its ability to outperform the market in a consistent, sustainable and ideally uncorrelated way.

In a way, the real, underpinning strategy of a credit work out "alpha player" is similar to the one of a principal investors—or alternative asset manager, who seeks continuously to beat through time. If a credit work out is really good, e.g. is a solid and robust "alpha player", it can choose and offer to be paid for all of its services not with a fee but with a "cut" taken out of its overperformance vis a vis the market (e.g. market indexes of recovery or a benchmark of its main competitors). As a work out then takes a long position on the portfolios managed (and on their underlying collaterals), it tends to resemble the performance of an hedge fund—where the hedges are in this case its competitive advantages: borne out of talents, superior processes and procedures and algorithmics able to mine the data to know more, better and sooner that the rest of the market. Of course, a good view on the ways ahead of the economic cycle (or of its main subcomponents, such as the real estate cycle) will help the platform in recovering more and then share a greater part of generated value. But still, there will be opportunities to outperform the market also when the cycle is negative and the prices of collaterals are heading down—if real "alpha" capabilities are created.

In any case, we can summarize, going back to the very incipit of this book, it always pays to be an "alpha" player. And you may play different games and be many different things to be "alpha", but certainly—as we have discussed at length in the previous chapters, you need to follow an holistic and active approach, with decision—being WHAM with a "bang", as a notorious song of the eponymous pop band lead by the singer George Michael was suggesting, few decades in advance of the financial crisis and of its NPLs overflow.

Bibliography

Boland V (2014) How Ireland's NAMA moved centre stage. Financial Times (September)

Dziobek C, Pazarbasioglu C (1997) Lessons from the systemic bank restructuring: a survey of 24 countries. IMF Working Paper (December)

European Banking Authority (2012) Final draft on implementing technical standard (ITS) on supervisory reporting (Forbearance and non-performing exposures)

European Banking Coordination "Vienna" Initiative (2012) Working group on NPLs in Central, Eastern and Southeastern Europe

European Securities and Markets Authority (2012) Treatment of forbearance practices in IFRS Financial Statements of Financial Institutions

Hawkins J, Turner P (1999) Bank restructuring in practice. BIS Policy Papers (August)

Kawalec S (2002) Different models of bad debt restructuring. International seminar on comparative experiences in confronting banking sector problems in Central/Eastern Europe and Central Asia (April)

Klein N (2013) Non-performing loans in CESEE: determinants and impact on macroeconomic performance. IMF Working Papers (March)

Noonan L (2014) Ireland's NAMA sets 2016 target to redeem 80 pct of bonds from banks. Reuters (December)

Rottke N, Gentgen J (2006) Workout management of non-performing loans: a formal model based on transaction cost economics. J Property Investment Finance 26(1):59–79 (October)

Sanderson R, Politi J (2014) Italy considers bank reforms package to clean up bad loans. Financial Times (February)

Scardovi C (2009) Asymmetric information, market failures and bad banks: international experiences and proposals for Italy. Bancaria. n 11/2009, pp 70–83

Vagnoni G, Galloni A (2014) Italia accelera su piano bad bank per sciogliere nodo sofferenze. Reuters (February)

C. Scardovi, *Holistic Active Management of Non-Performing Loans*,
DOI 10.1007/978-3-319-25363-3